GENES & DISEASE

SICKLE CELL DISEASE

GENES & DISEASE

GENES & DISEASE

SICKLE CELL DISEASE

Phill Jones

An imprint of Infobase Publishing

Chelsea House
An imprint of Infobase Publishing
132 West 31st Street
New York NY 10001

Library of Congress Cataloging-in-Publication Data

Jones, Phill, 1953-
   Sickle cell disease / Phill Jones.
      p. cm.—(Genes and disease)
   Includes bibliographical references and index.
   ISBN 978–0-7910–9587–4 (hardcover)
   1. Sickle cell anemia—Popular works. I. Title. II. Series.

   RC641.7.S5J67 2008
   616.1'527—dc22   2008004959

Chelsea House books are available at special discounts when purchased in bulk quantities for businesses, associations, institutions, or sales promotions. Please call our Special Sales Department in New York at (212) 967–8800 or (800) 322–8755.

You can find Chelsea House on the World Wide Web at
http://www.chelseahouse.com

Text design by Annie O'Donnell
Cover design by Ben Peterson

Printed in the United States of America

Bang NMSG 10 9 8 7 6 5 4 3 2 1

This book is printed on acid-free paper.

All links and Web addresses were checked and verified to be correct at the time of publication. Because of the dynamic nature of the Web, some addresses and links may have changed since publication and may no longer be valid.

CONTENTS

1

THE MEDICAL DETECTIVES

Walter Clement Noel was born and raised on Grenada, an island in the Caribbean Sea. He enjoyed a life of privilege. His mother had inherited the Duquesne Estate, located in mountainous bush country at the north end of the island. The family home perched on top of a hill that overlooked a plantation.

Noel attended Harrison College on the Caribbean island of Barbados. At the age of 20, Noel decided to continue his education in the United States. He wanted to be a dentist. This was in June or July of 1904.

On September 15, 1904, the *SS Cearense* docked in New York. Noel was on board, and he had a medical problem—a sore on his ankle had become very painful. A doctor treated the wound with iodine. The sore healed, leaving a scar. Noel might not have cared about the scar. His legs were covered with scars from old ulcers.

Noel continued his trip to Illinois. On October 5, he began classes at the Chicago College of Dental Surgery. Around Thanksgiving Day, however, Noel developed another medical problem. This time, he had trouble breathing. On December 26, Noel walked across the street from his rented room to Presbyterian Hospital. Here, he met Dr. Ernest E. Irons, a 27-year-old intern.

7

Irons learned that his patient had been reluctant to exercise for the past three years. Noel found any physical exertion difficult. For about a year, Noel had noticed shortness of breath, which he thought might have been caused by excessive smoking. When Noel developed chills, fever, weakness, dizziness, and a bad cough, he decided to seek help at the hospital.

The doctor performed routine medical examinations and lab tests, including a microscopic examination of Noel's blood. Irons discovered that his patient had a deficiency of red blood cells—a condition called **anemia**. The doctor also found something unusual in the blood: Some of the red blood cells were pear-shaped or elongated. Normal red blood cells have the shape of a **biconcave** disk, which is like a doughnut with a pushed-in center instead of a hole. Irons told his superior, Dr. James B. Herrick, about the strange blood cells. They did not realize it yet, but the doctors had discovered a new disease.

Two circumstances made the discovery of the new blood disease possible. One involved American history. In January 1865, following the end of the American Civil War, Congress and the president put into effect the Thirteenth Amendment, a law that abolished slavery. The new law freed 4 million black people. Eventually, opportunities arose for former slaves and their children to attend medical and dental schools, especially in the northern states. By the early 1900s, Chicago had a growing population of African American healthcare professionals. One of the city's dental schools had accepted Walter Clement Noel, a black student from Grenada.

The second circumstance was that Noel came under the care of two doctors who had an interest in blood and blood disorders. In particular, Herrick believed that diagnosis of an illness could be aided by an examination of a patient's

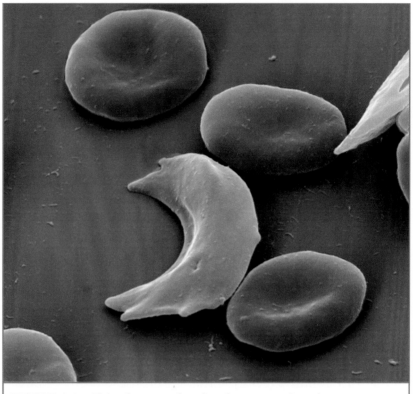

FIGURE 1.1   This photograph taken by a scanning electron microscope shows the elongated shape of a sickled cell.

blood with a microscope. By the time Noel visited the hospital, Herrick and Irons could prepare their own specimens for microscopic blood studies, and they knew how to interpret their findings. However, Noel's blood was a mystery because it contained so many thin, elongated red blood cells.

They treated Noel with food, rest, and syrup of the iodide of iron, a mixture used to treat anemia. Noel regained his strength and the number of normal-looking red cells in his blood increased. He left the hospital after four weeks.

Noel continued his studies at the dental school. Several times, Herrick and Irons treated Noel at the hospital for severe stomach pain, chills, fever, weakness, back pains, sore arm muscles, and other problems. Each time, they noticed the strange, elongated red blood cells in Noel's blood.

In May 1907, Noel graduated dental school and returned to Grenada. He started a dental practice and lived above his office. On May 2, 1916, Noel became very ill from **pneumonia**, a disorder of the lungs that can be caused by infection. He did not recover and died at the age of 32. Death at an early age was not unusual in his family. Noel's father had died from a kidney disease at the age of 36. Jane, Noel's sister, had died when she was 24. Her doctor had decided that weakness from a lung disease had caused Jane's death.

Herrick published an article about Noel's visits to his hospital in the November 1910 issue of the *Archives of Internal Medicine*. In the first sentence, Herrick explained why he decided to write the article. "This case is reported," Herrick wrote, "because of the unusual blood findings, no duplicate of which I have ever seen described." He suggested that an unknown change within Noel's red blood cells caused the bizarre, crescent-shaped forms. "The question of diagnosis," he concluded, "must remain an open one unless reports of other similar cases with the same peculiar blood-picture shall clear up this feature."

Although Herrick could not diagnose Noel's illness, his report prompted other doctors to recognize a similar blood disorder in their patients. A pattern began to emerge.

MORE CLUES ABOUT THE MYSTERIOUS ILLNESS IN THE BLOOD

Ellen Anthony, an African American, was born around 1885 and grew up in the farmland of Campbell County, Virginia. Like Noel's family, the Anthony family experienced ill health. Ellen Anthony's father had a kidney disease, four brothers and three sisters died in childhood, and a fourth sister died as a young adult from an undiagnosed brain illness.

Anthony and Walter Noel shared another common experience: recurring sickness. When Anthony had the strength, she worked as a cook and housekeeper. Otherwise, she suffered from pneumonia, severe stomach pain, chills, fever, nosebleeds, and shortness of breath. In April 1909, she became a patient at the University of Virginia Hospital. This had been her third visit to the hospital. Clinicians were puzzled by the odd shapes of her blood cells. The most common was a crescent shape.

The doctors sent a sample of Anthony's blood to specialists at the Johns Hopkins University Hospital in Maryland. The specialists decided that Anthony had an unusual type of anemia. They did not think that the findings in the blood were evidence of a new disease.

In October 1910, Anthony could no longer work due to shortness of breath. She was admitted to the hospital on October 25. Benjamin Earl Washburn, a fourth year medical student, was chosen to take care of her. Within weeks, the *Archives of Internal Medicine* journal carried James Herrick's article about Walter Clement Noel and his oddly shaped blood cells. The report on Noel might have prompted Washburn to write about Ellen Anthony's case. Washburn's article appeared in the February 1911 issue of the *Virginia Medical Semi-Monthly*. Like Herrick, Washburn admitted that he could not provide a diagnosis of his patient's condition. Little is known about Anthony, except that she regained her health and left the hospital. Historians have also learned that she had to return to the hospital at least eight more times.

Soon, a report about a third patient with strange blood cells gave doctors a clue that Noel and Anthony had a new type of disease. The third patient was a 21-year-old woman from St. Louis, Missouri, who had recurring skin ulcers and anemia. Like Noel and Anthony, the woman had a black ancestry. The woman was the only remaining child in the family; her two brothers and a sister had died at early ages. The family doctor had found that the children had severe anemia.

In a 1915 issue of the *Archives of Internal Medicine*, the patient's doctors, Jerome E. Cook and Jerome Meyer of Washington University Medical School, explained that they had compared the clinical symptoms of their patient with those reported for Noel and Anthony. "We are forced to the conclusion," they wrote, "that we have in these three cases a group which belongs quite apart from anything heretofore described." In short, they thought that they had found a new type of disease. Cook and Meyer also suggested that the new disease might be inherited, because three of their patient's siblings had died from severe anemia.

Dr. Victor Emmel, a professor of anatomy, theorized that people with the newly discovered blood disease did not make both normal red blood cells and sickle-shaped cells. Instead, he thought that the normal cells might transform into a sickle shape while the cells circulated in the bloodstream.

To test his theory, Emmel obtained blood samples from Cook and Meyer's patient and from the patient's father. He sealed blood samples between glass slides and allowed them to sit at room temperature. The patient's blood sample contained normal red blood cells and crescent-shaped cells. In time, the patient's normal red blood cells became crescent-shaped. At first, the blood sample of the patient's father seemed to have only normal blood cells. While the blood sat at room temperature, some of the father's cells also turned crescent-shaped. These observations suggested that the ability of the patient's red blood cells to change form had been inherited from her father.

Emmel's experiments changed the way that doctors looked at the three patients. Before the experiments, they had grouped the patients together because of their similar symptoms. Now, the focus turned to the patients' blood. Emmel suggested that a diagnosis of the disorder—whatever it might be—could be based upon an examination of the blood alone. Independent of symptoms, the disease could be characterized by sickle-shaped red blood cells.

OVERCOMING SICKLE CELL ANEMIA SYMPTOMS

Tionne "T-Boz" Watkins grew up in Iowa. She was not a healthy child; her classmates called her "Sicko." When she was eight years old, a doctor explained why she had been so weak: She had sickle cell anemia. The doctor predicted that Tionne would depend upon disability benefits for her entire life. Tionne proved the doctor wrong about that.

Tionne's singing, dancing, and songwriting made her a star. She became one of three performers in the music group TLC. One of the best selling female rhythm and blues groups of all time, TLC earned numerous honors, including four Grammy Awards.

The Sickle Cell Disease Association of America Inc. invited Tionne to be their spokesperson, and she agreed. Since then, the organization has credited her with educating the public about the disease and for inspiring those who have sickle cell anemia.

The organization's Web site displays a letter from Tionne about her struggles. "I have learned to smile when I wasn't happy," she wrote, "to sing when I didn't feel like it, and to do things just to please my fans." Tionne also wrote about her attitude. She had decided to face her illness and to make the best of it.

On March 15, 1915, a 21-year-old African American man was admitted to Johns Hopkins Hospital. He said that he was weak and that he had been weak and sickly his entire life. An examination of his blood revealed that he had anemia and that a large number of red blood cells had a sickle shape.

Dr. Verne R. Mason published a report about the fourth patient in 1922. The doctor gave the new disease a name: **sickle cell anemia**. Mason stressed that the disease was inherited. He was correct about that, but he incorrectly suggested that sickle cell anemia occurs only in people of African descent. This misconception lasted decades.

Now, researchers focused on the sickle-shaped red blood cells. The odd cells might cause the many symptoms experienced by patients. But what caused red blood cells to change their shape?

THE FIRST MOLECULAR DISEASE

Red blood cells contain a very large number of **hemoglobin** molecules, the iron-containing molecules that carry oxygen throughout the body. Hemoglobin has two components: a **protein** and a **heme group**. The protein is a large, globular molecule, whereas the heme group is a smaller molecule that acts as a framework to hold an iron atom, which binds oxygen.

When researchers examined red blood cells from an individual with sickle cell anemia, they saw that the cells appeared as normal biconcave disks when the blood contained adequate oxygen. If they decreased the amount of oxygen in the blood sample, the cells turned crescent shaped and the hemoglobin appeared to form a mass. These findings suggested that the sickling alteration of red blood cells might be connected with hemoglobin.

In 1946, Linus Pauling of the California Institute of Technology, or Caltech, assigned to a student named Harvey Itano a challenging task: Explore the chemistry of hemoglobin and its relationship, if any, to the sickling transformation. Itano's project was to examine the physical and chemical properties of hemoglobin molecules from red blood cells of people with sickle cell anemia and compare them with the hemoglobin molecules found in the cells of normal, healthy individuals.

Early studies focused on the heme group because it binds oxygen. Little came from these efforts. Next, Itano turned to the protein part of hemoglobin. In 1948, he proposed to examine hemoglobin protein using a new method called **electrophoresis**. This technique used electric currents to explore the chemistry of proteins.

The basic idea of the technique is that proteins, like many biological molecules, contain atoms that have negative charges, positive charges, or no charge. The balance of negative and positive charges determines the overall charge on a particular protein.

As an example, consider a Protein A that has 40 negative charges and 30 positive charges, and a Protein B that has 59 negative charges and 79 positive charges. One negative charge cancels one positive charge. Consequently, Protein A would have a net charge of -10 (30 positive charges plus 40 negative charges), and Protein B would have a net charge of +20 (79 positive charges plus 59 negative charges).

In electrophoresis, an electric field acts on charged proteins and causes them to move. The distance that a protein moves in the electric field depends upon the protein's net charge.

The Caltech researchers performed electrophoresis experiments with hemoglobin from sickle cell anemia patients and from healthy individuals. They discovered that the two proteins differed in net charge. The scientists suggested that sickle cell anemia hemoglobin may have two to four more positive charges than normal hemoglobin. They also suggested that the difference in charge caused sickle cell hemoglobin molecules to bind together when red blood cells were exposed to low oxygen levels.

In other words, they proposed a cause for sickle cell anemia. If a person has the disorder, then the red blood cells contain a type of hemoglobin with a net charge that differs from normal hemoglobin. The difference in the sickle cell hemoglobin's net charge causes the proteins to clump together when exposed to low oxygen levels. As sickle cell hemoglobin molecules gather together, they form a mass that causes the red blood cell to change shape.

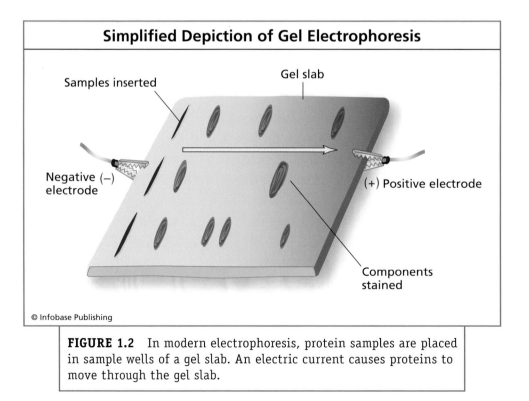

FIGURE 1.2   In modern electrophoresis, protein samples are placed in sample wells of a gel slab. An electric current causes proteins to move through the gel slab.

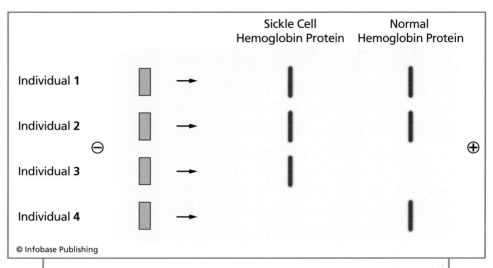

FIGURE 1.3 This drawing of an electrophoresis gel shows the proteins of four people. The appearance of dark stains under two possible protein categories reveals whether or not these people have sickle cell traits in their genes. Individuals 1 and 2 carry the sickle cell trait in their genes, but do not have sickle cell anemia. Individual 3 has sickle cell disease. Individual 4 does not carry the trait or have the disease.

The Caltech researchers published their findings in a 1949 *Science* paper entitled "Sickle Cell Anemia, a Molecular Disease." They had found an abnormality in the chemistry of a protein that seemed to cause a disease.

SICKLE CELL ANEMIA TODAY

According to the Sickle Cell Disease Association of America Inc., more than 70,000 people in the United States have sickle cell anemia. The United States is not alone. People who have sickle cell anemia live in many parts of the world, including Africa, Europe, and India. Healthcare organizations consider sickle cell anemia to be an international health problem.

AN ANCIENT POINT OF VIEW ON SICKLE CELL ANEMIA

In 1910, James B. Herrick published his report about Walter Clement Noel's illness. This marked the first account of sickle cell anemia in Western medical literature. Reports about other patients soon appeared in medical journals. Physicians began to highlight sickled red blood cells as the hallmark of the disease.

American doctors found out about sickle cell anemia during the early twentieth century. Yet the disease has been known in Africa for thousands of years. Traditional African names for sickle cell anemia reflect the painful symptoms of the disease. Among four African tribes, the disease was named *chwechweechwe*, *nwiiwii*, *nuiduidui*, and *ahotutuo*. The names mean "beaten up," "body biting," "body chewing," and "painful body."

Sickle-shaped blood cells can decrease and even block blood flow throughout the body, causing severe pain and damaging the lungs, kidneys, and other organs. Due to their abnormal shape, these blood cells are fragile and tend to break apart. The mass destruction of red blood cells causes anemia, one of the conditions noted by Dr. Ernest E. Irons when he examined Walter Clement Noel.

Scientists eventually learned that normal hemoglobin and sickle cell hemoglobin differ to a very small extent, amounting to a change of less than 0.2% in protein weight. Yet this tiny change has a large effect on the life of a person who has sickle cell hemoglobin.

2

CELLS: THE BODY'S PROTEIN FACTORIES

Sickle cell anemia is caused by a very small change in the structure of one protein. Even though the change is very small, the altered protein severely affects how the body functions. The change in function can be seen in the many symptoms that can be caused by sickle cell anemia.

Good health depends upon a group of body systems that perform certain functions. In a way, the body is like a computer. The proper function of a computer depends upon the actions of its systems. Does the computer produce quality sound? If it does, then it has a good audio system. Does the computer store information reliably? If so, then the operating system and hard drive must be in good shape. The ability to enter data relies upon an input system that can include a keyboard and a mouse. The ability to retrieve data depends upon an output system that can include a monitor and a printer. The ability to keep in touch with friends on their computers relies upon a communications system that connects the computer to an Internet service provider and the Internet.

The health of the human body also relies on a group of systems that work together. Consider the act of walking. This action depends upon the coordination of at least five systems:

- Muscles of the muscular system work against the rigid bones of the skeletal system.
- The nervous system sends electrical signals to leg and arm muscles.
- The lungs of the respiratory system and the heart and blood vessels of the circulatory system supply the oxygen needs of muscle tissue. Working muscles produce waste products. One type of waste product is a gas called carbon dioxide. Carbon dioxide is carried in the blood to the lungs, where it is exhaled from the body.

The health of the human body requires balance. It is like a pyramid formed by acrobats. To maintain the pyramid, every acrobat must perform a role to steady the structure. If one acrobat fails, then the entire pyramid collapses. Similarly, the failure of one of the body's systems can cause ill health. In sickle cell anemia, the circulatory system does not perform its role. When the circulatory system fails, health problems arise in many other systems of the body.

Each system of the body is also like a human pyramid. A biological system requires the proper function of organs and tissues. In turn, organs and tissues rely upon the proper function of cells.

A TRIP INSIDE A MAMMALIAN CELL

A cell is the basic building block of human tissues. One cell can function independently of other cells. A cell can also interact with other cells to perform a task. Muscle cells, for example, work together to produce movement.

A cell contains small structures that perform functions vital to the cell's survival. These structures act like small organs and thus are called **organelles**. A cell's organelles float in a jellylike mix of water and proteins called **cytosol**.

Animal Cell

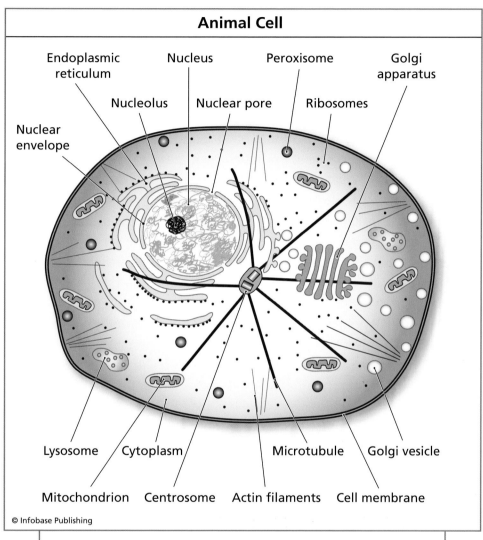

Endoplasmic reticulum   Nucleus   Peroxisome   Golgi apparatus

Nucleolus   Nuclear pore   Ribosomes

Nuclear envelope

Lysosome   Cytoplasm   Microtubule   Golgi vesicle

Mitochondrion   Centrosome   Actin filaments   Cell membrane

FIGURE 2.1   The structure of the animal cell reveals a complex array of organelles suspended in cytosol and enclosed by the cell membrane.

Cells are surrounded by a cell membrane that keeps the contents of the cell separate from the environment. The membrane also controls the movement of material into and out of the cell.

The normal operation of a human body depends upon a division of labor. These jobs are shared among the body's systems. A cell also relies upon a division of labor. Many jobs are assigned to the cell's organelles.

One type of organelle is a collection of folded membranes called the **endoplasmic reticulum**. It is here that the cell synthesizes many proteins. **Mitochondria** are also organelles. Mitochondria are shaped like tiny jellybeans with internal membranes. They also have a key job; they break down sugars to supply energy to the cell.

A cell is like a factory. A product (protein) is made in the endoplasmic reticulum. Mitochondria power the process of making protein. In a factory, managers make decisions about what the factory should produce. Managers are the factory's command center. A cell also has a command center. It is located in a structure called the **nucleus**. The nucleus stores genetic material that instructs the cell to make certain proteins. A membrane called the nuclear envelope surrounds the nucleus and keeps the genetic material inside the nucleus.

The nuclear envelope separates the nucleus from other parts of the cell. In fact, the inside of a mammalian cell can be considered to have two basic parts: a nucleus and **cytoplasm**. Cytoplasm is simply the cytosol and organelles found outside the nucleus.

The nucleus cannot be totally isolated from the cytoplasm. After all, the nucleus is the command center. Pores in the nuclear envelope allow certain molecules to leave the nucleus. These molecules carry instructions from the genetic material to the protein-making machinery.

The instructions of the genetic material are stored in a compound called **deoxyribonucleic acid** (**DNA**). Typically, the DNA in a nucleus can be found in the form of **chromatin**. Chromatin is a mixture of proteins, DNA, and other nucleic

DNA Structure

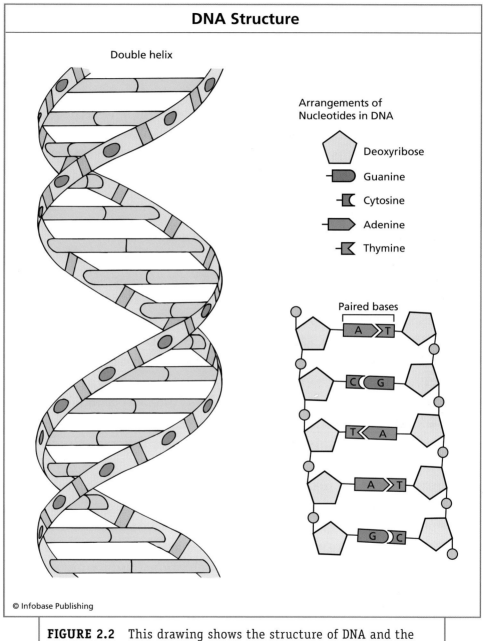

Double helix

Arrangements of
Nucleotides in DNA

Deoxyribose

Guanine

Cytosine

Adenine

Thymine

Paired bases

A — T

C — G

T — A

A — T

G — C

FIGURE 2.2   This drawing shows the structure of DNA and the pairing of the nitrogenous bases that make up the double helix formation.

acids. Under the microscope, chromatin has a wiry, fuzzy appearance. When a cell is getting ready to reproduce by splitting into two cells, the chromatin compacts into rodlike structures called **chromosomes**.

Most human cells typically have 46 chromosomes. The DNA in the chromosomes determines whether a person will have brown eyes or blue eyes, will have red hair or brown hair, or will be male or female. The DNA contains the complete set of instructions for an individual's body.

THE DNA HELIX: A CASE OF MOLECULAR ATTRACTION

In human cells, DNA takes the form of two DNA strands that wrap around each other. This structure, the familiar double helix, looks like a spiral staircase. Each DNA molecule is made of chemical compounds called **nucleotides**. Each nucleotide has three parts: (1) a sugar molecule, (2) a chemical group that contains phosphorus, and (3) a molecule called a **base**, which contains nitrogen.

A DNA molecule is a **polymer**. A polymer is a large chemical made by combining smaller units. A polymer is like a train. A train is formed by combining small units: cars. A DNA molecule is also formed by combining small units: nucleotides. In a train, cars are coupled to each other. In a DNA molecule, nucleotides form chemical bonds with each other. The sugar group of one nucleotide binds with the phosphate group of another nucleotide. This means that a DNA molecule has a "sugar-phosphate-sugar-phosphate" structure. The structure is called the sugar-phosphate backbone of DNA.

The bases of nucleotides stick out from the sugar-phosphate backbone. A DNA molecule has four types of

A POLYMER THAT STOPS BULLETS

Polymers are chains made of similar or identical groups called **monomers**. A protein has monomers of amino acids, and DNA has monomers of nucleotides. Starch is another type of polymer that occurs in nature. Starch has monomers of glucose molecules.

The world is full of synthetic polymers. Plastic is one type of a synthetic polymer. Just to name a small number of examples, synthetic polymers can be found in frying pans (Teflon), clothes (polyester), disposable cups (polystyrene), bicycle tires (rubber), plastic bags (polyethylene), carpets (polyolefin), and inline skates (polyurethane).

One type of synthetic polymer can be woven into material five times stronger than steel on an equal weight basis. Police wear the material in lightweight body armor to stop bullets. Windsurfing sails of this material can withstand 60-mile (97-kilometer)-per-hour winds. Ropes made of this material secured the Mars Pathfinder to the airbags in its landing apparatus. The polymer in the material is Kevlar.

One Kevlar polymer strand can have up to a million monomers linked together. A collection of Kevlar strands can be imagined as a bundle of very thin, long needles. These polymer strands are strong by themselves. However, the unique strength of Kevlar comes from the chemical bonding between the strands to form a polymer network.

When a bullet strikes Kevlar body armor, the impact causes polymer strands to elongate like the strands of a spider's web. The elongation of Kevlar strands causes other strands of the polymer network to move, dissipating the bullet's energy. The fiber network quickly absorbs the energy delivered by a speeding bullet.

Double Helix

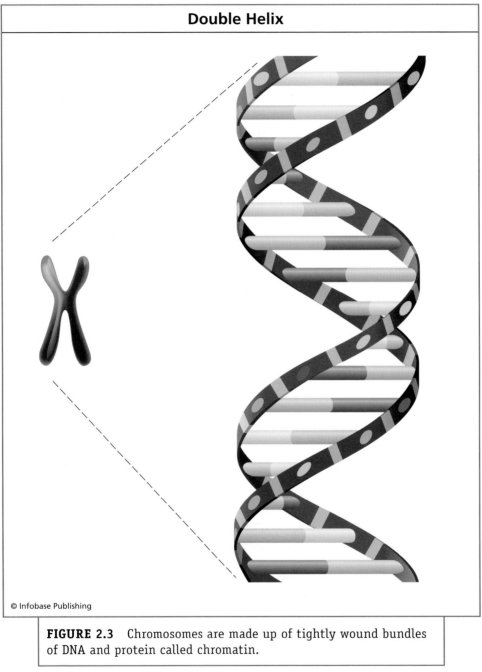

FIGURE 2.3   Chromosomes are made up of tightly wound bundles of DNA and protein called chromatin.

bases: adenine, cytosine, guanine, and thymine. Scientists refer to the bases by the first letter of their names. For example, "AGCTGA" indicates a short strand of DNA that has the base sequence "adenine-guanine-cytosine-thymine-guanine-adenine."

DNA can take the shape of a double helix. Why do the two strands of DNA stay together? The answer is that certain bases are attracted to each other. This attraction can be imagined as a type of magnetic attraction. The rules of attraction are simple: An A on one strand pairs with a T on the other strand, and a G on one strand pairs with a C on the other strand. When bases of two different DNA strands bind together, they form a **base pair**.

Consider a very short DNA molecule with two strands. One strand has the following sequence: "CATTAGCATGGACT." The other strand would have the sequence "GTAATCGTACCTGA." Together, the strands would appear as follows:

CATTAGCATGGACT
GTAATCGTACCTGA

This is so because the first C in CATTAGCATGGACT pairs with the G in GTAATCGTACCTGA, the A in CATTAGCATGGACT pairs with the T in GTAATCGTACCTGA, and so on.

In humans, the complete set of genetic instructions found in the cell nucleus, the human **genome**, amounts to about three billion base pairs. This huge amount of DNA includes 20,000 to 25,000 genes.

A **gene** is a DNA nucleotide sequence that provides the information a cell needs to synthesize a protein. A protein, like a DNA molecule, is a polymer made by combining smaller units.

Although DNA and proteins are polymers, they are made from very different building blocks. The building blocks of a protein are not nucleotides, but rather molecules called **amino acids**. Mammals produce proteins using 20 different amino acids. DNA has only four types of nucleotides that instruct the cell to build a protein with 20 types of amino acids in mammals. How is this achieved? The instructions of DNA take the form of a code.

THE GENETIC CODE

Computers also operate by reading a code. Computers read a code that is a group of 0s and 1s. A short string of computer code might appear as:

001100111001010101011001011101001.

This string of 0s and 1s looks like nonsense. It really does not make sense by itself. But computers do not read code simply as a group of 0s and 1s. Instead, a computer divides a series of numbers into segments. Many computers bundle a series of 0s and 1s into groups of eight called bytes. Such a computer would read the above series of numbers as four distinct units:

00110011 10010101 01011001 01101001.

By dividing a series of 0s and 1s into bundles of eight, computer programmers created a code. This code has over 250 distinct bytes of 0s and 1s. The bytes function as words to provide instructions for the computer.

While computer programmers are clever, nature devised this type of coding system first. DNA uses a similar approach in the **genetic code**. Consider the following short nucleotide sequence:

AACCACCCAGAAGGAGCA.

Instead of breaking the sequence into bundles of eight like a computer, the genetic code uses groups of three nucleotides. A group of three nucleotides, called a **codon**, directs a cell to add a particular amino acid to a chain of amino acids to produce a protein. For example, the above nucleotide sequence is read as:

AAC CAC CCA GAA GGA GCA.

These six codons instruct the protein-making machinery to add amino acids called asparagine, histidine, proline, glutamic acid, glycine, and alanine.

The Genetic Code

Second letter

First letter		U	C	A	G	Third letter
U	UUU UUC	Phenyl-alanine	UCU UCC UCA UCG — Serine	UAU UAC — Tyrosine	UGU UGC — Cysteine	U C
	UUA UUG	Leucine		UAA Stop codon / UAG Stop codon	UGA Stop codon / UGG Tryptophan	A G
C	CUU CUC CUA CUG	Leucine	CCU CCC CCA CCG — Proline	CAU CAC — Histidine	CGU CGC CGA CGG — Arginine	U C
				CAA CAG — Glutamine		A G
A	AUU AUC AUA	Isoleucine	ACU ACC ACA ACG — Threonine	AAU AAC — Asparagine	AGU AGC — Serine	U C
	AUG	Methionine		AAA AAG — Lysine	AGA AGG — Arginine	A G
G	GUU GUC GUA GUG	Valine	GCU GCC GCA GCG — Alanine	GAU GAC — Aspartic acid	GGU GGC GGA GGG — Glycine	U C
				GAA GAG — Glutamic acid		A G

© Infobase Publishing

FIGURE 2.4 The above table provides a visual guide to how different combinations of the four nucleotides in DNA direct the formation of different amino acids.

The scientists who cracked the genetic code achieved a great breakthrough in science. In 1968, Robert W. Holley, Har Gobind Khorana, and Marshall W. Nirenberg shared the Nobel Prize for interpreting the genetic code and discovering its role in protein synthesis. After the discovery of the genetic code, scientists could "read" genes. That is, a scientist can study the nucleotide sequence of a gene and predict the amino acid sequence of the protein that the gene encodes.

SOME HISTORICAL BACKGROUND FOR MODERN GENETICS

Interpretation of the genetic code rested on the many experiments that scientists had performed for 100 years. It all started with a monk. In the 1860s, an Austrian monk named Gregor Mendel performed breeding experiments with pea plants. He studied how parent plants passed certain characteristics, such as flower color, to their offspring. Mendel suggested that the parent plants passed on "invisible factors" to their young. The invisible factors caused the offspring to inherit characteristics in a predictable way. Today, the invisible factors are called genes.

In the 1940s, George Beadle and Edward Tatum produced mutations in bread mold to study the relationship between genes and proteins. They concluded that each gene is responsible for directing a cell to make a specific protein.

Around the same time, Oswald Avery and his colleagues searched for the material that transformed harmless bacteria into pneumonia-causing bacteria in laboratory mice. They found that the material was DNA. They proposed that DNA transferred genetic information.

In the 1950s, James Watson and Francis Crick investigated the structure of DNA. They showed that DNA has the

TRICKING BACTERIA TO MAKE INSULIN

A very important feature of the genetic code is that the same code is used by almost all forms of life on Earth. Scientists use the code to synthesize DNA molecules that encode human proteins. These synthetic genes can be transferred to bacterial cells, transforming the cells into human protein-producing factories. One of the first human proteins produced in bacteria was the hormone insulin.

Normally, a mammal makes insulin in an organ called the pancreas. Insulin is a vital hormone that regulates blood glucose levels. If the pancreas does not make insulin, the person develops diabetes.

During the late 1970s, scientists devised a way to transfer a synthetic human insulin gene into a bacterium called *Escherichia coli*, or *E. coli*. Scientists chose bacteria to make human insulin because bacteria reproduce at a very fast rate. A bacterial cell reproduces by splitting into two cells. Each of these split into two cells, creating four cells. The four cells split to form eight cells, and so on. In this way, one *E. coli* cell can produce about 17 million offspring cells during an eight-hour period. If the parent *E. coli* carries a synthetic human insulin gene, then its offspring should also carry copies of the insulin gene and make insulin.

Today, human insulin is produced in fermentation vessels that hold thousands of gallons of *E. coli*. Yeast cells in which a human gene has been inserted also make human insulin. The use of gene technology to manufacture insulin for use by diabetics has virtually replaced the traditional method of isolating insulin from the pancreases of cows and pigs. Insulin is not unique in this way. Biotech companies produce over 100 therapeutic proteins in huge vats of bacteria, yeast, or mammalian cells.

form of a double helix. They also proposed that cells might make molecules that copy the instructions found in a DNA strand. These molecules would leave the cell's nucleus and carry genetic information to the cell's protein-making machinery. The research of Holley, Khorana, and Nirenberg revealed the genetic code and its function in protein synthesis.

DNA AND RNA

A cell's machinery for producing proteins is usually found outside the nucleus and in the membranes of the endoplasmic reticulum. Since nuclear DNA stays in the nucleus, the cell must have a way to transfer the genetic information contained in a DNA molecule to the protein-producing machinery. People use messengers to pass on coded messages. Cells also have messengers. Cells transfer DNA's messages using molecules of **ribonucleic acid** (**RNA**).

An RNA molecule is similar to a DNA molecule, but RNA and DNA differ in three ways. First, DNA contains the sugar *deoxy*ribose, whereas RNA contains the sugar ribose. This is why one is called DNA and the other is called RNA. Second, RNA usually exists in the form of a single strand, rather than the typical double-stranded helix of DNA. Third, RNA has a base called uracil (U) that takes the place of the thymine (T) found in DNA.

The special type of RNA molecule that carries DNA's genetic information out of the nucleus to the cell's protein-making machinery is called **messenger RNA**, or **mRNA**. Messenger RNA has a nucleotide sequence that is a copy of the nucleotide sequence found in one strand of a DNA molecule. Of course, a messenger RNA molecule will not be an exact copy of a DNA molecule's nucleotide sequence, because DNA contains thymine while RNA contains uracil.

The genetic code is based on RNA's uracil system. For example, a very small fragment of DNA that encodes a protein might have the nucleotide sequence of "AGA TGT CCT ATA." The copy of this sequence in a messenger RNA molecule would be "AGA UGU CCU AUA."

Any code must tell a reader when to start and stop reading the coded message. In the genetic code, the codon "AUG" signals the addition of the amino acid methionine. This codon also signals the start of protein synthesis. There are three codons that do not instruct the cell to add an amino acid. Instead, these three codons (UAA, UAG, and UGA) instruct the cell to stop adding amino acids.

The process of making an RNA copy of a gene is called **transcription**, because the cell transcribes (or copies) DNA. The process of making a protein using the information in messenger RNA is called **translation**. The cell translates the code of a messenger RNA molecule into a string of amino acids that will make a protein.

MOLECULAR WORKOUT: AMINO ACIDS GET PROTEIN INTO SHAPE

It is handy to imagine protein synthesis as adding amino acid "cars" to a growing protein "train." However, a protein does not have the form of a linear train. Amino acids push and pull a protein into a shape. For example, a protein can have a spiral shape, the shape of a knot, or a combination of these shapes.

The 20 different amino acids that are found in proteins have two basic parts. One part is identical in all amino acids. The identical component allows amino acids to couple with each other like train cars. The other part differs among the amino acids and is called a side group. One way to picture a protein is to imagine the identical parts of amino acids forming a chain. Each amino acid has a side group that sticks out from the chain.

The sequence of amino acids determines a protein's shape in the watery environment of a cell. For example, some side groups are hydrophobic (water-fearing). These move away from water and toward a protein's dry interior. Hydrophobic groups act like the head of scared turtle, ducking inside the shell. Other side groups are hydrophilic (water-loving). These side groups move away from the protein's interior to the watery exterior of a protein. Other side groups are attracted to each other and bend the protein to move closer together.

Amino acid side groups are like a collection of bratty children. They all want something and will do what is necessary to get their way. As amino acid side groups move to get their way, they bend and fold the protein. Their combined activities determine a protein's shape. The shape of a protein is critical, since a protein's shape determines its function.

Just how important is a particular sequence of amino acids? One amino acid change in the 146 amino acids of a hemoglobin molecule causes hemoglobin to contort into an abnormal shape. The unusual shape destroys the normal function of hemoglobin and severely affects health. This is the basis of sickle cell anemia.

3

NORMAL AND MUTANT HEMOGLOBINS

Blood contains cells and plasma, a yellowish-colored liquid that consists mostly of water. The plasma helps to transport nutrients and waste products throughout the body. The typical color of blood is due to the presence of red blood cells, the most common type of cell found in blood. One drop of blood holds millions of red blood cells.

A red blood cell appears red because it is full of hemoglobin protein. Hemoglobin contains iron, which binds with oxygen. Oxygen molecules attach to hemoglobin as red blood cells move through the lungs. When red blood cells reach the body tissues where the oxygen level is low, hemoglobin releases oxygen and picks up carbon dioxide. Back in the lungs, hemoglobin releases its carbon dioxide and picks up oxygen. Carbon dioxide leaves the body in the exhaled air.

DEVELOPMENT OF RED BLOOD CELLS

The human body begins its lifelong production of red blood cells even before birth. An early fetus makes red blood cells in the spleen and liver. As a fetus matures, marrow tissues in bone cavities take over the job of producing red blood cells. After birth, the **bone marrow** retains its job as the main producer of red blood cells. During childhood and through adult life, the bone marrow is the source of new blood cells.

A red blood cell develops in stages. The development of a blood cell begins with a **pluripotential stem cell**. A cell that is "pluripotential" can transform into many types of cells. In bone marrow, these stem cells can mature along a pathway that ends with a red blood cell. As the cell develops into a red blood cell, it ejects its nucleus, possibly to make room for the 200 to 300 million hemoglobin molecules that a typical red blood cell carries. When the cell reaches a stage called a **reticulocyte**, it leaves the bone marrow and enters the bloodstream. As a reticulocyte makes the final change into a mature red blood cell, it loses the last bits of its nucleus.

A red blood cell survives for about 120 days before it gets worn out. Two organs—the spleen and liver—remove old or damaged cells from the blood. The body reuses parts of damaged red blood cells, including hemoglobin.

In 1910, when Dr. James Herrick published his article on Walter Clement Noel, Herrick reported that Noel's blood had many red blood cells with nuclei. Since a human red blood cell normally lacks a nucleus, why should Noel have nucleated red blood cells? It is a matter of rushing production of red blood cells. A person with sickle cell anemia has fragile, crescent-shaped blood cells circulating in the bloodstream. These abnormal cells do not live as long as normal red blood cells. The increased destruction of red blood cells causes anemia. To compensate for the loss of red blood cells, the bone marrow boosts its production of new red blood cells. As a result, many cells are pushed into the bloodstream before they are mature. The immature cells still contain nuclei.

THE HEMOGLOBIN MOLECULE

Hemoglobin consists of two types of molecules: heme and protein. Heme is a fairly flat molecule that has an iron atom connected to a ring of nitrogen atoms. It is the iron atom that binds an oxygen atom.

A hemoglobin molecule contains two types of a globular protein called a **globin**. In adults, the major form of hemoglobin, **hemoglobin A**, has two alpha globin proteins and two beta globin proteins. The **alpha globin** protein has 141 amino acids, whereas the **beta globin** protein has 146 amino acids.

The assembly of a hemoglobin molecule is complex. First, each globin protein must bind with a heme group. Then, four globins with their heme groups combine to form a spherical hemoglobin molecule. Since a hemoglobin molecule has four proteins, each with its own heme group, the molecule has four binding sites for oxygen. Hemoglobins are very effective at binding with the oxygen molecules that diffuse through a red blood cell. The binding of the first oxygen molecule to a heme group causes a change in the hemoglobin's shape. The change in shape assists the binding of oxygen molecules to the remaining three heme groups.

Although humans produce different types of hemoglobin molecules before birth and after birth, each consists of four protein chains. In the fetus, the major form of hemoglobin, **hemoglobin F**, has two alpha globin proteins and two gamma globin proteins. The synthesis of gamma globin protein decreases around the time of birth. At the same time, the synthesis of beta globin protein increases. This replacement of gamma globin synthesis with beta globin synthesis enables the production of hemoglobin A. After infancy, most humans have only very small amounts of hemoglobin F.

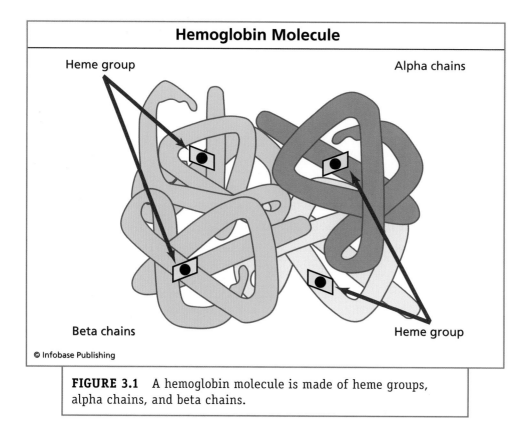

Hemoglobin Molecule

Heme group

Alpha chains

Beta chains

Heme group

© Infobase Publishing

FIGURE 3.1   A hemoglobin molecule is made of heme groups, alpha chains, and beta chains.

The body switches from hemoglobin F to hemoglobin A because birth changes the source of oxygen. Before birth, hemoglobin in fetal red blood cells obtains oxygen from the mother's blood as it passes through the placenta. Hemoglobin F must compete with maternal hemoglobin A for oxygen molecules. Hemoglobin F competes by binding oxygen molecules more efficiently than hemoglobin A. After birth, red blood cells carry hemoglobin through the oxygen-rich tissues of the lungs, where oxygen is readily available.

The red blood cells of a person who has sickle cell anemia carry a type of hemoglobin that is neither hemoglobin A nor hemoglobin F.

BLOOD SUBSTITUTES

In August 2002, a California police officer and his canine partner, Saxon, cornered a suspect in front of the suspect's house. The suspect ran to the front door, and K-9 Officer Saxon followed in hot pursuit. When the police officer reached the door, he had to dodge a shotgun blast. After a second blast, Saxon staggered out of the house and collapsed. Shotgun pellets had peppered the police dog's chest and legs. Although Saxon lost a lot of blood, treatment with Oxyglobin, a blood substitute, saved the dog's life.

Compounds like Oxyglobin are often described as a "blood substitute" or "artificial blood." However, "oxygen therapeutic" is a more accurate term. Unlike true blood, an oxygen therapeutic does not fight an infection or help to heal a wound. An oxygen therapeutic has only one purpose: to deliver oxygen to the body's tissues.

In theory, purified hemoglobin could be injected into the bloodstream to help deliver oxygen to tissues. However, this does not work in practice, because when removed from a red blood cell, hemoglobin can fall apart into its four proteins.

A chemical treatment can prevent this from happening. The treatment stabilizes hemoglobin by linking the four proteins, and even by linking several hemoglobin molecules. This chemical treatment acts like a bungee cord that binds books together. Oxyglobin is made from cattle hemoglobin that has been treated to link hemoglobin molecules. Scientists are developing similar oxygen therapeutics with pig hemoglobin and hemoglobin isolated from donated human blood.

Chemically treated hemoglobin binds oxygen in much the same way that hemoglobin binds oxygen in a red blood cell. A

(continues)

(continued)

very different type of oxygen therapeutic uses chemicals called perfluorocarbons (PFCs) to carry oxygen.

Oxygen readily dissolves in a PFC solution and oxygen-starved tissues can easily acquire oxygen from PFCs. Companies are working on PFC mixtures that can be injected into blood vessels. The PFCs pick up oxygen from the lungs and transport oxygen to the body's tissues. A person who receives a PFC mixture may have to wear an oxygen mask, because PFCs are less efficient oxygen carriers than hemoglobin.

ALTERED STRUCTURE OF SICKLE CELL HEMOGLOBIN

In 1949, Harvey Itano and his coworkers announced that they had found a chemical difference between normal hemoglobin and sickle cell hemoglobin. Using the technique of electrophoresis, they showed that the two proteins differ in their net charge. Sickle cell hemoglobin, they proposed, might have two to four more positive charges than normal hemoglobin. The difference in charge suggested that normal hemoglobin and sickle cell hemoglobin differ slightly in their amino acid sequences.

During the fall of 1952, Dr. Vernon M. Ingram obtained a job as a protein biochemist in the Medical Research Council Unit at the University of Cambridge in England. He worked in a laboratory next to the office of Francis Crick, one of the scientists who discovered the double helix structure of DNA. Ingram was working on methods to analyze the protein structure of hemoglobin. Crick suggested that

Ingram might want to compare normal hemoglobin with sickle cell hemoglobin.

Ingram decided to tackle the project by cutting each hemoglobin molecule into fragments and examining the chemical behavior of the protein fragments. His goal was to find only one fragment that differed between normal and sickle cell hemoglobin molecules. This fragment would contain the key to the differences between the two types of hemoglobin.

To cut hemoglobin into pieces, he treated hemoglobin molecules with trypsin, an enzyme that digests proteins. Trypsin digestion cleaved hemoglobin into about 26 peptides. A **peptide** is simply a chain of amino acids that is smaller than a protein.

Ingram spotted samples of digested hemoglobin molecules onto a wet sheet of paper. He then applied an electric current to perform electrophoresis. Under the influence of the electric current, hemoglobin peptides moved along the paper. To further separate the peptides, he turned the paper at a right angle and used the technique of **chromatography**.

Chromatography separates molecules made from different chemicals. In paper chromatography, a sample of molecules is forced to move across a sheet of paper. Molecules that bind more tightly with paper tend to move more slowly than molecules that bind weakly with paper. In Ingram's experiment, peptides with charged amino acids tended to bind more tightly to the paper and moved more slowly than peptides that had fewer charged amino acids.

After treating the paper with a chemical to stain the peptides, Ingram had a pattern of hemoglobin peptides that was like a fingerprint. That is, two samples of the same protein treated in the same way should produce the same patterns of peptides. On the other hand, two samples of different proteins should produce distinct peptide patterns.

Ingram's technique revealed that a peptide in sickle cell hemoglobin was more positively charged than the corresponding peptide in normal hemoglobin. Further studies showed that the sickle cell hemoglobin peptide contained less of the amino acid glutamic acid and more of the amimo acid valine. This suggested that a valine replaced a glutamic acid in the sickle cell hemoglobin peptide. Ingram and his colleagues also found that the peptide

DIFFERENT TYPES OF HEMOGLOBIN DISEASES

Inherited hemoglobin diseases occur in various forms. In one type of hemoglobin disease, a mutant hemoglobin gene encodes an altered version of a hemoglobin protein. A change in amino acid sequence modifies the properties of the protein. Researchers have found more than 700 hemoglobin proteins that differ in amino acid sequence from normal hemoglobin. Yet only the sickle cell beta globin protein and two other altered hemoglobin proteins commonly occur in humans.

A second type of hemoglobin disease occurs when a gene mutation causes a decrease in the synthesis of normal alpha globin or beta globin hemoglobin proteins. Reduced hemoglobin protein synthesis causes an inadequate supply of hemoglobin and may even shorten the life of red blood cells. A hemoglobin disease caused by impaired hemoglobin protein synthesis is called a **thalassemia**. The main symptom of thalassemia is anemia.

Thalassemia is one of the most common types of genetic disorders in the world. Every year, according to the March of had been cut from an end of the beta globin protein of the hemoglobin molecule.

These studies of sickle cell hemoglobin had great meaning for molecular biology. Scientists knew that a person inherits sickle cell anemia from their parents. Genetic studies suggested that sickle cell anemia is caused by a **mutation** in one gene. One type of mutation involves a change in the nucleotide sequence of a DNA molecule. Ingram's studies showed that the difference between normal hemoglobin and sickle cell hemoglobin is caused by the replacement of a

Dimes group, about 100,000 babies are born with severe forms of thalassemia worldwide.

In the United States, Cooley's anemia is the most common, severe form of thalassemia. The disease was named after Thomas Cooley, the doctor who first described the disorder in 1925. Cooley's anemia is caused by a complete lack of beta globin synthesis. A person who has this disease needs frequent blood transfusions to survive.

A third type of hemoglobin disease is caused by a mixture of abnormal globin proteins and mutations that alter the synthesis of normal globin proteins. A disease called sickle beta thalassemia falls into this group. This disease occurs when a person inherits a sickle cell beta globin gene from one parent and a gene that encodes normal beta globin from the other parent. Unfortunately, a mutation impairs synthesis of the normal beta globin protein. When cells fail to make normal beta globin, hemoglobin molecules only contain the sickle cell form of beta globin. The patient's illness becomes almost identical to that of a person with sickle cell anemia.

single amino acid. This meant that the mutation of one gene changed the amino acid sequence of a particular protein. In other words, the nucleotide sequence of a gene determines the amino acid sequence of a protein.

Scientists wondered about the type of gene mutation that led to the production of sickle cell hemoglobin. It would take about 20 years before techniques became available to answer this question. During the mid-1970s, scientists developed methods for identifying the sequence of nucleotides in a single strand of DNA. Soon, researchers used these techniques to sequence the beta globin genes. They found that the gene encoding the beta globin of sickle cell hemoglobin has a single nucleotide difference, compared with the gene encoding the beta globin of normal hemoglobin. The

Normal Hemoglobin

Nucleotide	CTG	ACT	CCT	GAG	GAG	AAG	TCT
Amino acid	Leu	Thr	Pro	Glu	Glu	Lys	Ser
	|			|			|
	3			6			9

Sickle Cell Hemoglobin

Nucleotide	CTG	ACT	CCT	GTG	GAG	AAG	TCT
Amino acid	Leu	Thr	Pro	Val	Glu	Lys	Ser
	|			|			|
	3			6			9

© Infobase Publishing

FIGURE 3.2   The beta globins of normal hemoglobin and sickle cell hemoglobin differ at the sixth amino acid. Notice that a single nucleotide mutation causes the amino acid substitution.

sixth codon of sickle cell beta globin reads "GTG" rather than "GAG," which is the sixth codon of normal beta globin. This single nucleotide mutation accounts for the amino acid change found in sickle cell hemoglobin.

ALTERED FUNCTION OF SICKLE CELL HEMOGLOBIN

How can the change of one amino acid affect the function of the entire hemoglobin molecule? Recall that amino acids have two basic parts. One part, which is the same in all amino acids, allows amino acids to bind together. The other part differs among the amino acids and is called a side group. The sequence of amino acids—with their side groups—determines the shape of a protein.

Researchers found that the sixth amino acid of normal beta globin is a glutamic acid molecule. Glutamic acid has a net charge of −1 and is hydrophilic. In the beta globin of sickle cell hemoglobin, glutamic acid is replaced by valine, an amino acid that has a net charge of 0 and is hydrophobic. The differences in the chemical properties of valine and glutamic acid affect the way that the beta globin of hemoglobin folds and interacts with other proteins. A change in the structure of the two beta globins of a hemoglobin protein alters the function of the hemoglobin molecule.

In a red blood cell, beta globins of one sickle cell hemoglobin molecule can bind with beta globins of other sickle cell hemoglobin molecules. The proteins tend to bind with each other, because hydrophobic valine seeks out a dry region in another beta globin. As sickle cell hemoglobin molecules bind together, they form a long chain. Hemoglobin chains bind together, creating large, rigid, ropelike structures. The process of building a large molecule from smaller

components should seem familiar. It is the process of polymerization, and it is the key to symptoms experienced by a
person who has sickle cell anemia.

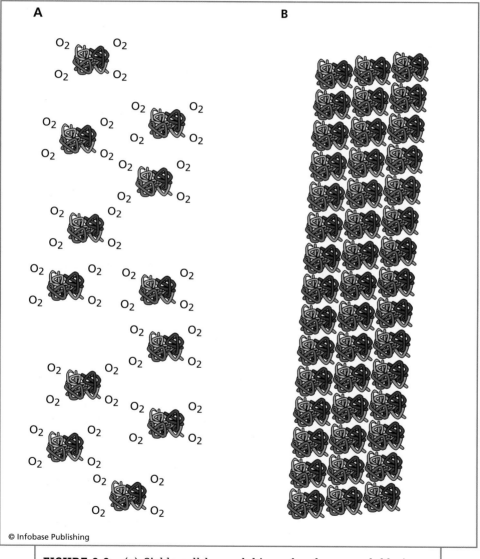

FIGURE 3.3 (a) Sickle cell hemoglobin molecules are soluble in
a cell if the hemoglobin molecules bind oxygen. (b) If sickle cell
hemoglobin molecules lack bound oxygen, then the hemoglobin
molecules bind with each other, or polymerize.

As hemoglobin molecules polymerize, the rigid rope-like forms distort the shape of the red blood cell. Cells with polymerized hemoglobin molecules appear elongated and can take on a crescent shape. Polymerization of sickle cell hemoglobin is a reversible process. Under conditions of low oxygen, a sickle cell contains polymerized hemoglobin molecules. When the cell passes through the lungs—an area of plentiful oxygen—hemoglobin polymerization is reversed, because the hemoglobin molecules bind oxygen and change their shape. When a sickle cell hemoglobin molecule carries oxygen bound to its heme groups, the hemoglobin's beta globins are not in a good position to bind with another sickle cell hemoglobin molecule. In a person with sickle cell anemia, a red blood cell shifts back and forth from a normal, flexible biconcave disk to a rigid, fragile elongated form.

SICKLE CELL ANEMIA, SICKLE CELL DISEASE, AND THE SICKLE CELL TRAIT

Doctors use two terms when describing sickle cell disorders. Sickle cell anemia and **sickle cell disease** do not mean the same thing. The difference lies in the genes. A person inherits two genes for beta globin protein—one gene from each parent. The genes may be identical or they may be different. Suppose that a child inherits a sickle cell beta globin gene from the father and a normal beta globin gene from the mother. In this case, the child will have red blood cells that contain a mixture of sickle cell hemoglobin and normal hemoglobin. People who have a sickle cell beta globin gene and a normal beta globin gene are said to have the **sickle cell trait**. According to the Sickle Cell Disease Association of America Inc., about 2.5 million people in America have the sickle cell trait.

What happens when a child inherits sickle cell beta globin genes from the father *and* from the mother? The child can only produce sickle cell hemoglobin in the red blood cells. This person has sickle cell anemia.

Sickle cell disease is caused by the inheritance of a sickle cell beta globin gene and a second abnormal beta globin gene. If that second abnormal beta globin gene is also a sickle cell beta globin gene, then the sickle cell disease is sickle cell anemia.

Here is another way to think about these terms. Scientists use the symbol "Hb A" to indicate normal hemoglobin protein and "Hb S" to represent **hemoglobin S**, which is sickle cell hemoglobin. Suppose that an examination of hemoglobin from three people reveals that one has Hb A alone, one has Hb A and Hb S, and one has Hb S alone. The results indicate the following about these people:

- Hb A only: This person neither carries the sickle cell trait nor has sickle cell anemia.
- Hb A plus Hb S: This person carries the sickle cell trait, but does not have sickle cell anemia.
- Hb S only: This person has sickle cell anemia.

In the United States, sickle cell anemia accounts for the majority of sickle cell disease, and sickle cell anemia has the severest symptoms of any of the sickle cell diseases.

4

HOW SICKLE CELL HEMOGLOBIN AFFECTS HEALTH

The circulatory system is a vital and hard-working part of the human body. On average, the circulatory system of an adult human body transports about 5 liters of blood every one or two minutes. The circulatory system has three key parts: blood, the heart, and blood vessels. Blood travels through the vessels, removing toxic waste products and delivering oxygen. Blood picks up its supply of oxygen while flowing through the lungs. After blood leaves the lungs, it enters the heart. The left side of the heart pumps the blood into the aorta, which is a type of blood vessel called an **artery**. Arteries are strong blood vessels. They have to be tough to stand up to the high pressure of blood pumped from the heart. The aorta is the largest artery in the body. From the aorta, the arteries divide and subdivide, forming smaller vessels.

The oxygen-rich blood from lungs travels through a network of smaller and smaller arteries until it passes through the smallest blood vessels, which are called **capillaries**. Normal red blood cells are flexible. Their ability to bend and twist becomes important when they travel through narrow capillaries.

Capillaries can be thinner than a strand of hair, and they also have extremely thin walls. Oxygen and nutrients in the blood pass through capillary walls into the cells of the body. At the same time, carbon dioxide and other waste products from the cells pass through the thin capillary walls and into the blood.

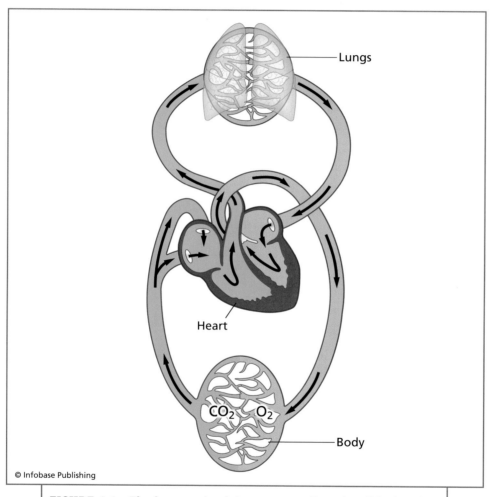

FIGURE 4.1 The human circulatory system. In veins *(blue),* red blood cells contain little oxygen. The cells pick up oxygen as they travel through the lungs. The heart pumps oxygenated blood *(tan)* into the arteries. From the arteries, the blood passes through narrow capillaries and into veins for the return trip to the lungs.

From the capillaries, blood travels into a network of blood vessels that merge, forming larger and larger vessels, which are called **veins**. Veins have thinner walls than arteries. Veins do not need to be as strong as arteries, because the blood pressure in veins is lower than that in the arteries. Blood travels through the veins back to the heart. From the right side of the heart, blood enters the pulmonary artery, which carries it to the lungs. In the lungs, carbon dioxide passes out of the blood and oxygen enters the blood, and the cycle starts again.

BIOLOGICAL EFFECTS OF THE SICKLE CELL MUTATION

Red blood cells rush into the vessels of the circulatory system, delivering oxygen and removing carbon dioxide. Thanks to a flexible cell membrane, these cells bend and twist as they hurtle through small blood vessels. Sickle cell anemia changes this.

Sickle cell hemoglobin forces red blood cells to undergo a transformation. When sickle cell hemoglobin gives up oxygen, hemoglobin molecules polymerize, forming long, rope-like structures. Red blood cells lose their disk shape, along with their elasticity. The cells assume an inflexible, crescent shape, the form of a sickled red blood cell.

Sickled red blood cells do not bend and twist as they speed through narrow blood vessels. Instead, they tend to clog vessels. This effect of sickled cells is called **vaso-occlusion**, which simply means obstruction of blood vessels. At one time, scientists thought that sickled red blood cells blocked small vessels because the cells lacked the flexibility of normal red blood cells. That is, sickled cells could not pass through tiny blood vessels and piled up like cars in front of a narrow tunnel. As it turns out, vaso-occlusion is more complicated than a car pileup.

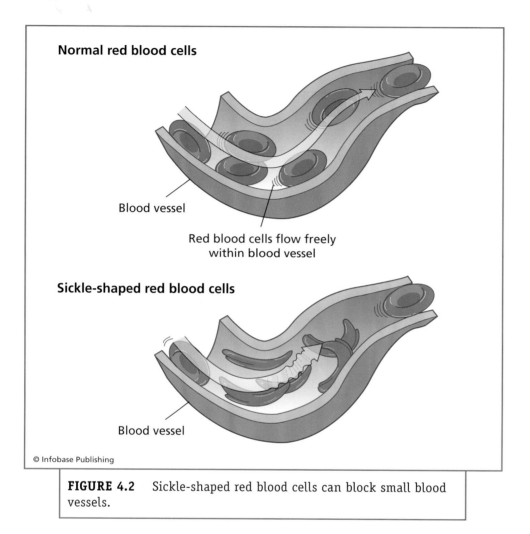

Normal red blood cells

Blood vessel

Red blood cells flow freely
within blood vessel

Sickle-shaped red blood cells

Blood vessel

© Infobase Publishing

FIGURE 4.2   Sickle-shaped red blood cells can block small blood
vessels.

In sickle cell anemia, sickled red blood cells cling to the
inner wall of small veins. Why should the cells stick to veins
rather than arteries? Red blood cells, and the hemoglobin
molecules inside, are full of oxygen as they travel through
arteries. The cells give up their oxygen as they pass through
capillaries. By the time they move through small veins,
sickle cell hemoglobin molecules carry little or no oxygen.

Without oxygen, sickle cell hemoglobin polymerizes, and cells take on the sickle shape.

When sickled red blood cells start to cling to blood vessel walls, they begin a chain reaction. If a sickled red blood cell can travel back to the lungs and pick up oxygen, the polymerized hemoglobin breaks apart. But a blockage of small blood vessels slows the cell's return to the lungs. The delay provides more time for sickle cell hemoglobin to polymerize and create more sickled cells. As more sickled blood cells cling to the vessel walls, nearby tissues becomes starved for oxygen—a condition called **hypoxia** (low oxygen).

Sickle cell hemoglobin polymers have another effect on the red blood cell. Polymerization damages the cell membrane. A red blood cell with a damaged membrane can have a permanently deformed shape. Damage to the cell membrane also allows water molecules to rush out of the cell. As the red blood cell loses water, it becomes dehydrated and dense.

When a red blood cell shrinks, its volume decreases. Even though the cell becomes smaller, it contains the same amount of sickle cell hemoglobin. As a result, hemoglobin molecules are pushed together and this promotes more hemoglobin polymerization. The red blood cell's loss of water cannot be fully reversed. Eventually, the cell becomes so dehydrated that it cannot change from a deformed shape back into a normal biconcave disk. These dense red blood cells with their abnormal shapes contribute to vaso-occlusion.

Dehydration adds yet another type of stress to red blood cells. The cells already experience stressful cycles of hemoglobin polymerization and the breakdown of hemoglobin polymers. These stressed, sickled cells have a short life. The early destruction of red blood cells causes anemia.

Sickle Cell Anemia Symptoms

People who have sickle cell anemia do not all endure the same types and frequency of symptoms. Starting in early childhood, some patients must receive regular treatments in a hospital. Others have very few symptoms through adult life. Most sickle cell symptoms are caused by a blockage in the blood flow that damages the body's tissues. Pain associated with damaged, oxygen-starved tissues is the most common symptom. It accounts for the majority of hospitalizations. Young children can develop painful swellings in their hands

HEMOGLOBIN GETS ATTITUDE AT HIGH ALTITUDE

Humans live at many different elevations across the globe. Since ancient times, people have lived in South America's Andean Mountains on land located 13,000 feet (4 kilometers) above sea level. When settlers first arrived there, they probably suffered from hypoxia, which is also known as mountain sickness. Headaches, vomiting, and weakness are symptoms of this disorder. It is the thin air that causes mountain sickness. At high altitudes, a volume of air contains fewer oxygen molecules than the same volume at sea level.

Normal breathing of thin air cannot provide enough oxygen to supply the body's tissues. The people of the Andes can live at high altitudes because they have more hemoglobin in their blood cells. As a result, their blood can transport more oxygen than the blood of a typical person who lives at sea level.

The Andeans are not unique. The human body adjusts to the low oxygen found at altitudes above 6,500 feet (2 km). Within several days at this height, a person begins to breathe faster, and the heart rate increases to pump oxygen-carrying blood to and feet. Older people may experience pain in the head, chest, stomach, and back. The blockage of blood vessels and the resulting oxygen starvation can injure vital organs, including the spleen, lungs, kidneys, bones, and brain:

♦ **Spleen.** The spleen removes old red blood cells and helps to fight infections by destroying bacteria and viruses. To perform these jobs, the spleen has an extensive system of capillaries (the smallest blood vessels). The narrow vessels

tissues. As weeks pass, the heart rate slows to a speed closer to normal, while the bone marrow produces extra red blood cells. The body changes in other ways to help a person survive with less oxygen in the air.

Athletes can make good use of an extra supply of red blood cells. The bonus cells could deliver more oxygen to straining muscles and perhaps boost an athlete's performance. This idea inspired altitude training for athletes who compete in events that require endurance.

In the traditional training method, athletes stayed at camps located over 8,200 feet (2.5 km) above sea level. Today, altitude training can be achieved at sea level using a special, closed sleeping tent. By adjusting the amount of oxygen in the air that flows into the tent, trainers can imitate altitudes up to 10,000 feet (3 km) and above.

Following altitude training, levels of red blood cells stay elevated for several weeks. The success of the training, however, varies greatly among athletes.

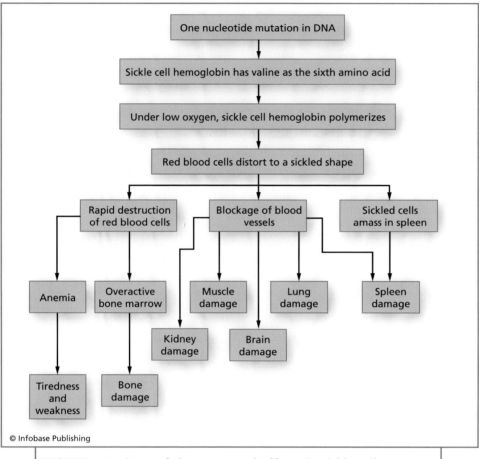

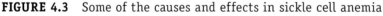

FIGURE 4.3   Some of the causes and effects in sickle cell anemia

are susceptible to blockage by sickled red blood cells. The blockage deprives the spleen of oxygen, injures cells, and impairs the spleen's function. Having a damaged spleen increases the risk of bacterial and viral infections.

◆ **Lungs.** Persons with sickle cell anemia have a tendency to get lung infections, particularly pneumonia, which can be caused by bacteria or viruses. Both children and adults with sickle cell anemia are prone to pneumonia. Pneumonia can cause a life-threatening illness called acute chest syndrome, which causes fever, chest pain, cough, and trouble breathing.

◆ **Kidney.** The two kidneys filter blood, removing waste products produced by the cells. If the kidneys stop working, toxic chemicals build up in the bloodstream. The kidneys are another type of organ that can become damaged in a person with sickle cell anemia.

◆ **Bones.** In sickle cell anemia, the body tries to make up for the constant loss of red blood cells. Abnormally large amounts of bone marrow form to produce new red blood cells. The massive bone marrow tissue may create pressure that can damage bones. Packed bone marrow also slows blood flow, which encourages the change of red blood cells to the sickle shape and the blockage of blood vessels. The blockage prevents infection-fighting cells from reaching the bone marrow to battle viruses and bacteria.

◆ **Brain.** Damage to the blood vessels in the brain can cause many types of symptoms. These include severe headaches, a change in behavior, and a **stroke**—a sudden loss of blood to the brain. A stroke is one of the most disastrous symptoms of sickle cell anemia.

When a body organ fails, the ill effects can multiply and create new problems. For example, sickled blood cells can damage the spleen, which impairs the spleen's ability to fight infections. This increases the chance that bone marrow will become infected. Certain viruses infect bone marrow and disrupt the production of new red blood cells. A

ANTARCTIC ICEFISH: LIFE WITHOUT HEMOGLOBIN

Tucked inside a red blood cell, hemoglobin shuttles oxygen from the environment to tissues. It also carries waste carbon dioxide from tissues to the environment. Hemoglobin plays a vital role in sustaining the lives of mammals, fishes, birds, reptiles, and amphibians. As a rule, a loss of hemoglobin can cause an animal to become sick or die. Nature, however, has exceptions to rules. Certain Antarctic icefish are exceptions when it comes to hemoglobin. They do not have hemoglobin. They do not even have red blood cells.

In December 1953, Johan Ruud visited South Georgia, a sub-Antarctic island surrounded by icy waters. During his trip, he studied the strange, almost colorless blood of the blackfin icefish. Ruud learned that the fish's blood lacked red blood cells and hemoglobin. Three other types of icefish also had colorless blood. How does the icefish survive without hemoglobin? The answer lies in the water.

Water can hold dissolved gases, such as oxygen. Cold water retains more dissolved oxygen than warm water. The Antarctic icefish lives in constantly frigid water that is full of oxygen.

As the icefish swims through the chilly water, dissolved oxygen travels through the icefish's gills and into the bloodstream. The blood carries dissolved oxygen to the fish's oxygen-starved tissues. To ensure an ample supply of oxygen, the icefish has a hefty, strong heart that forcefully pumps a large volume of blood through its circulatory system.

Scientists have studied the DNA of two types of icefish. They found that the fishes' DNA lacks the genes that encode the hemoglobin proteins, alpha globin and beta globin. Researchers propose that icefish gradually lost their alpha and beta globin genes in the course of their evolution.

person with sickle cell anemia already has red blood cells with short lives. If a virus prevents the formation of new red blood cells, then the number of red blood cells falls to a critically low level, causing severe anemia.

Sickle cell anemia represents a chain of cause and effect events. The mutation of one nucleotide in the beta globin gene causes a substitution of one amino acid in the beta globin protein. The amino acid replacement causes sickle cell hemoglobin molecules to polymerize. Hemoglobin polymerization alters the red blood cell shape and the functions of the cell membrane. These changes lead to the blockage of blood vessels and the early destruction of red blood cells. In turn, vaso-occlusion and the destruction of red blood cells cause the symptoms of sickle cell anemia.

The ill effects of sickle cell anemia take their toll on the human body. People with sickle cell anemia tend to have shorter lives than healthy people. In 1994, according to the World Health Organization, people who lived in the United States and had sickle cell anemia had an average lifespan of between 40 and 45 years. By 2003, medical care increased the average lifetime to 50 and over, according to Jennifer Bojanowski of the *Gale Encyclopedia of Medicine.*

Of course, these estimates are not true for everyone. The American Sickle Cell Anemia Association reports that the organization has patients in their sixties. The disease varies among patients: Two people with sickle cell anemia can experience different types and different frequencies of symptoms.

GENETICS OF
SICKLE CELL ANEMIA

Sickle cell anemia ranks as the most common type of inherited blood disorder in the United States. According to the National Institutes of Health, about 80,000 Americans have sickle cell anemia.

In 1922, Dr. Verne R. Mason suggested that sickle cell anemia occurs only in people of African descent. This is untrue. A sickle cell gene causes the disease. Inheritance of the gene is not limited to people of African descent. However, it is true that more copies of the sickle cell gene can be found among certain groups of people. According to the American Sickle Cell Anemia Association, the sickle cell gene occurs among Americans as follows:

- One in 500 African Americans has sickle cell anemia;
- One in 900 Hispanic Americans has sickle cell anemia;
- One in 58,000 Caucasian Americans has sickle cell anemia.

The reason for these differences can be found in history.

For years, scientists have studied sickle cell genes. They have found five types of the sickle cell beta globin gene. The five types of mutant genes differ from each other by small changes in nucleotide sequences in or near the gene. These changes in the DNA do not affect the amino acid sequence encoded by the sickle cell genes. Each sickle cell gene encodes the same mutant protein with a single amino acid change, compared with normal beta globin.

People living in particular regions of Africa—Benin, Cameroon, the Central African Republic (or Bantu), and Senegal—have four of the sickle cell gene types. Scientists propose that the mutations that created the versions of the sickle cell gene first arose in these regions.

The sickle cell gene did not remain in Africa. The slave trade forcibly removed Africans from their families and transported them across the globe. Historians suggest that the slave trade introduced the sickle cell gene into the Americas and the Caribbean islands. Normal human migration also dispersed the gene among various parts of the world. From Africa, the sickle cell gene spread to southern Europe. Today, many people in southern Europe carry the sickle cell gene, including Italians, Spaniards, Portuguese, and Greeks.

Scientists found the fifth type of sickle cell gene in people living in the Middle East and India. This sickle cell gene mutation may have first occurred in the Indus Valley people, one of the earliest civilizations of the Indian subcontinent. In time, this version of the sickle cell gene spread to people who lived in Middle East countries.

What is the significance of the five types of sickle cell gene? Scientists propose that the sickle cell gene mutation occurred in five different places and at five different times in human history. Why would a genetic mutation that causes

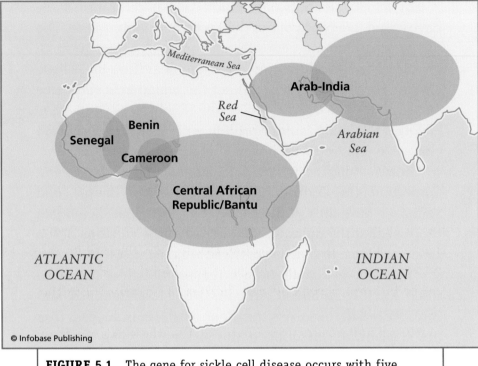

FIGURE 5.1   The gene for sickle cell disease occurs with five distinct variations. This suggests that the sickle cell mutation arose five different times in five different locations. The genetic variations are called by the names of their original locations: Senegal, Benin, the Central African Republic (or Bantu), Arab-India, and Cameroon.

ill health persist in the human race? A possible answer concerns mosquitoes.

THE SICKLE CELL GENE AND MOSQUITOES

In 1949, Dr. Anthony Allison, who grew up in Kenya, began a study on the sickle gene in Africa. He found something odd. A large number of people who lived near the Kenya coast and near Lake Victoria had the sickle cell trait. That is, they had one sickle cell beta globin gene and one normal beta globin gene. Yet, in the highlands between these areas, few people had the sickle cell trait. Allison wondered why the sickle cell gene had become common in certain areas of Kenya, but not in other areas.

Then, he realized that the Kenyan coast and Lake Victoria shared another factor in common. Both regions had a high rate of malaria caused by a parasite called *Plasmodium falciparum*. Malaria is a disease that can produce flu-like symptoms, severe medical problems, and even death. A mosquito infected with the parasite transmits it to humans while the insect feeds on blood. After entering a human's bloodstream, the parasite produces offspring. During one stage of its life cycle, the parasite reproduces in red blood cells. In time, the cells burst, releasing new hordes of parasites into the bloodstream.

Allison had a theory. He proposed that the sickle cell trait somehow allowed the red blood cells to resist the malaria parasite. In regions with a large number of parasite-carrying mosquitoes, a person who had the sickle cell trait had a better chance of survival than a person who had only normal beta globin genes.

Over the years, many studies have shown that Allison was correct. People who have the sickle cell trait are highly protected against severe malaria. When the parasite infects their red blood cells, knobs develop on the cell's outer cell membrane. The knobs cause the red blood cells to stick to the walls of small blood vessels. Due to low oxygen concentrations in the small vessels, the red blood cells compress into a sickle shape and kill the parasites inside the cells.

The defense offered by the sickle cell gene explains why the gene endured in the human race. In regions where malaria has been common, those who had no sickle cell gene risked life-threatening malaria. In contrast, people who had the sickle cell trait survived. These survivors passed the sickle cell gene on to their children. The sickle cell gene's protection against malaria has a cost, however. People who have two sickle cell genes have life-threatening sickle cell anemia.

GENETIC INHERITANCE

The sickle cell beta globin gene passes on from one generation to the next. Sometimes a child gets the sickle cell trait, sometimes a child gets sickle cell anemia, and sometimes

TRACKING THE TRAVELS OF ANCIENT HUMANS USING DNA

Identical twins have identical genomes. Otherwise, every person has a unique genome. The uniqueness of a person's genome can be found in a very small fraction of the DNA. Human DNA is 99.9% the same between any two people. The remaining 0.1% of the DNA includes genes that determine hair color, eye color, disease risk, and other traits. The tiny amount of DNA also includes nucleotide sequences with no known function.

Scientists have studied differences in nucleotide sequences that can be found in the 0.1% of human DNA. Some of these DNA variations, or **genetic markers**, have been part of human DNA since ancient times. These genetic markers can be found in the DNA of individuals from all ethnic groups.

Using DNA analysis, researchers traced the human species back to an ancient people who lived in East Africa. Most of the examined genetic markers developed during these ancient times.

About 50,000 to 60,000 years ago, humans began to travel from East Africa. Humans settled across the globe. As they a child gets two normal beta globin genes. The patterns of sickle cell beta globin gene inheritance may seem mysterious. Yet these patterns become easy to understand after learning how a person inherits a gene. It is time to explore how genes pass from one generation to the next.

Mitosis

Most of the body's cells reproduce by a method called **mitosis**. In mitosis, a cell duplicates its DNA and divides into two cells, known as **daughter cells**. The nucleus of each

adapted to their new lands, mutations created new genetic markers in human DNA. After finding a new home, people tended to stay there. They raised families in the land where they were born. In time, small differences in genetic markers developed among groups of humans who lived in different parts of the world.

A worldwide team of scientists has been searching for human genetic markers. They are testing DNA donated by more than 100,000 people. The scientists plan to use genetic markers to trace the journeys of ancient humans after they left Africa.

The huge DNA study has revealed the travels of ancient humans. For example, a mutation created one genetic marker ("M130") about 50,000 years ago. M130 first emerged in an African people. Early ancestors who had the M130 marker traveled along the African coastline. They crossed Arabia, India, and Southeast Asia. They also sailed to Australia. Around 10,000 years ago, their descendants left China or Russia and traveled to North America.

daughter cell carries the same genetic information as the nucleus of the original parent cell.

In humans, genetic information can be found in 3 billion base pairs of DNA. These nucleotide sequences are divided among 24 types of chromosomes:

- 22 chromosomes identified by number;
- An X chromosome and a Y chromosome.

The nucleus of human body cells contains 23 pairs of chromosomes, or 46 chromosomes. The nuclei of eggs in the female and sperm in the male each have only 23 chromosomes. The egg cell nucleus contains the 22 numbered chromosomes plus an X chromosome. The sperm cell contains the 22 numbered chromosomes plus a Y chromosome. When an egg and sperm fuse to form a new cell, that cell has the full complement of 46 chromosomes: 23 from each parent. A typical female has inherited one X chromosome from each parent, whereas a typical male has inherited an X chromosome from his mother and a Y chromosome from his father.

In mitosis, a cell prepares to divide by duplicating its DNA. Long molecules of DNA compress into chromosomes, which are then present in pairs. The membrane that surrounds the nucleus—the nuclear envelope—breaks down. Like strands of a spider's web, protein strings shoot out from two sides of the cell and attach to chromosomes. The pairs of chromosomes are separated when the protein strands pull chromosomes to opposite sides of the cell. Each side then has a copy of the cell's DNA. The cell membrane pinches into the middle of the cell, dividing it into two spheres. When the cell membrane meets itself in the middle of the cell, it splits the old cell into two cells. The nuclear envelope reforms in each cell.

Meiosis

Another type of cell division, **meiosis**, occurs only in the formation of eggs and sperm. The details of meiosis hold the key to understanding how people inherit the sickle cell beta globin gene.

There are two cell divisions in the course of meiosis, ultimately creating four daughter cells. The first division produces two cells from the original one. These two cells each divide to produce the four cells. Each of the four daughter cells contains 23 chromosomes, or half the number of chromosomes found in body cells (all cells other than eggs and sperm). If meiosis did not halve the number of chromosomes, then the number of chromosomes would double with each generation when the sperm and egg nuclei fuse.

The first stage of meiosis is similar to mitosis in that the DNA duplicates to create twice the number of chromosomes, and the nuclear membrane breaks down. Weblike proteins attach to chromosomes and pull them to opposite sides of the cell. An important difference between mitosis and meiosis concerns the way that the chromosomes separate. In mitosis, the chromosome pairs separate into two identical sets. In the first stage of meiosis, the chromosomes are not separated into two identical sets.

Consider a cell that contains only one type of chromosome, called chromosome 1. The cell would have two copies of the chromosome—one from the mother and one from the father. Call them chromosome 1m and chromosome 1f. The cell gets ready to divide, and DNA duplicates. Now, the cell contains two copies of chromosome 1m and two copies of chromosome 1f.

In mitosis, each side of the cell gets one copy of chromosome 1m and one copy of chromosome 1f. When the cell

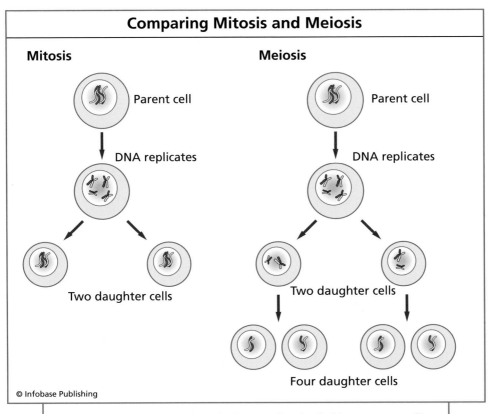

Comparing Mitosis and Meiosis

Mitosis

Parent cell

DNA replicates

Two daughter cells

Meiosis

Parent cell

DNA replicates

Two daughter cells

Four daughter cells

© Infobase Publishing

FIGURE 5.2 Mitosis and meiosis. In mitosis *(left)*, a parent cell divides to create two daughter cells, each with the full complement of DNA. In meiosis *(right)*, a parent cell divides twice, creating four daughter cells, each of which receives half the amount of DNA as the parent cell.

divides, the two daughter cells contain identical DNA. That is, each daughter cell has one copy of chromosome 1m and one copy of chromosome 1f.

Meiosis works differently. In the first stage of meiosis, each side of the cell gets two copies of chromosome 1m *or* two copies of chromosome 1f. When the cell divides, the daughter cells do not contain identical DNA.

What does this say about the first stage of meiosis in a human cell? Consider a female human cell. DNA duplicates to create the following chromosomes:

- Two copies of chromosomes 1 to 22 inherited from the mother;
- Two copies of chromosomes 1 to 22 inherited from the father;
- Two copies of the X chromosome inherited from the mother;
- Two copies of the X chromosome inherited from the father.

After the first stage of meiosis, each daughter cell will have two copies of chromosomes 1 to 22 and two copies of an X chromosome. Each cell contains some chromosomes inherited from the mother and some chromosomes inherited from the father.

To complete the picture, consider a male human cell dividing in the first stage of meiosis. In this case, DNA duplicates to create the following chromosomes:

- Two copies of chromosomes 1 to 22 inherited from the mother;
- Two copies of chromosomes 1 to 22 inherited from the father;
- Two copies of the X chromosome inherited from the mother;
- Two copies of the Y chromosome inherited from the father.

After the cell divides, each daughter cell will have two copies of chromosomes 1 to 22—some inherited from the father and some from the mother. One daughter cell will

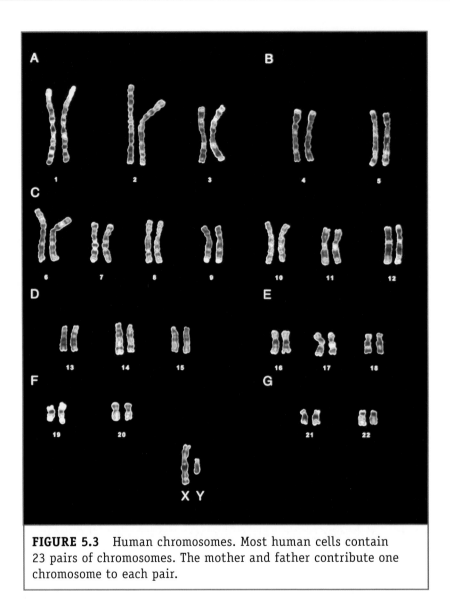

FIGURE 5.3   Human chromosomes. Most human cells contain 23 pairs of chromosomes. The mother and father contribute one chromosome to each pair.

contain two copies of the X chromosome and the other will contain two copies of the Y chromosome.

In the second stage of meiosis, each daughter cell divides its set of chromosomes equally between two cells, so that each cell contains the same DNA. Each of the four daughter cells contains half the number of chromosomes of the original cell. In males, the four cells develop into sperm cells, while in females, the cells develop into egg cells. Egg cells and sperm cells are also known as **gametes**.

PATTERNS OF INHERITANCE OF THE SICKLE CELL GENE

A person has two copies of the beta globin hemoglobin gene. One copy was inherited from the mother and one copy was inherited from the father. Meiosis separates the maternal and paternal copies of the beta globin genes. In a female, some eggs carry the maternal copy and some carry the paternal copy. Similarly, some of a male's sperm carry the maternal copy and some carry the paternal copy.

In thinking about the inheritance of the sickle cell gene, it can be helpful to focus on the three possible combinations of genes: (1) There can be two normal beta globin genes; (2) there can be one copy of the normal beta globin gene and one copy of the sickle cell beta globin gene—this person has the sickle cell trait; and (3) there can be two copies of the sickle cell beta globin gene—this person has sickle cell anemia.

People who have the sickle cell gene can pass it on to their children. Inheritance of the sickle cell gene follows predictable patterns. The patterns can be pictured as four possibilities. Before exploring these possibilities, recall that normal hemoglobin is also known as hemoglobin A. To simplify the examples, let "A" represent a copy of the normal beta globin gene and let "S" represent the sickle cell beta globin gene.

◆ **A person with two normal beta globin genes (*AA*) has children with a person who has two sickle cell genes (*SS*).** The person with two normal beta globin genes can only produce gametes

Sickle Cell Gene Inheritance Pattern

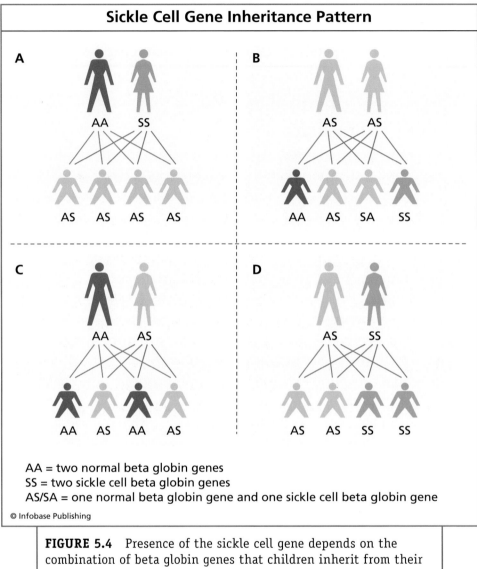

A

AA   SS

AS   AS   AS   AS

B

AS   AS

AA   AS   SA   SS

C

AA   AS

AA   AS   AA   AS

D

AS   SS

AS   AS   SS   SS

AA = two normal beta globin genes
SS = two sickle cell beta globin genes
AS/SA = one normal beta globin gene and one sickle cell beta globin gene

© Infobase Publishing

FIGURE 5.4   Presence of the sickle cell gene depends on the combination of beta globin genes that children inherit from their parents. Unless both parents carry only normal beta globin genes or only sickle cell beta globin genes, there can be a number of different potential outcomes for their children's genes.

that contain the normal version of the beta globin gene (*A*). Likewise, the person with two sickle cell beta globin genes produces only gametes that contain the sickle cell version of the beta globin gene (*S*). This means that all children should have one normal beta globin gene (*A*) and one sickle cell beta globin gene (*S*). The children would all have the sickle cell trait (*AS*).

- **Two people with the sickle cell trait (*AS*) have children.** Here, each person can produce two types of gametes. One type carries the normal beta globin gene (*A*); the other type of gamete carries the sickle cell beta globin gene (*S*). When gametes from these people combine, the possible outcomes are *AA, SS, SA,* and *AS.* That is, a child has a 50% chance of inheriting one copy of a normal beta globin gene with one copy of the sickle cell beta globin gene (*AS*), a 25% chance of inheriting two copies of the normal beta globin gene (*AA*), and a 25% chance of inheriting two copies of the sickle cell beta globin gene (*SS*).

- **One person has two normal beta globin genes (*AA*) and one person has the sickle cell trait (*AS*).** When gametes from these people combine, the possible outcomes are *AA, AA, AS,* and *AS.* In other words, each child has a 50% chance of inheriting two normal beta globin genes (*AA*). Each child also has a 50% chance of inheriting one normal beta globin gene and one sickle cell beta globin gene (*AS*).

- **One person has the sickle cell trait (*AS*) and one person has sickle cell anemia (*SS*).** When gametes from these people combine, the possible

WHAT ARE THE ODDS?

People deal with probabilities every day. What is the chance of rain? What are the odds that the bus will arrive on time? A probability indicates the chance that a random process will produce a certain outcome. Probability is calculated by comparing the number of ways that a particular outcome could occur against the number of possible outcomes. For example, pick a number from 1 to 20. What is the probability that the selected number is an even number? This range of numbers has 10 even numbers in a total of 20 numbers. The probability of picking an even number is 10 out of 20, which is 10/20, or 50%, or 0.5.

Sometimes, the outcome of one event affects the outcome of a second event. In these cases, the events are dependent. Suppose that a bag contains ten pieces of candy; one tastes like lemon and nine taste like broccoli. The probability of picking the lemon candy is 1 out of 10 (1/10, or 10%). Now, suppose that the selected candy is broccoli-flavored. Put it aside and try again. This time, the probability of picking the lemon candy is 1 out of 9 (1/9, or 11.1%). If the second selected candy is broccoli-flavored, put it aside. Try again. Each step in this process affects the outcome of the next step.

Events are independent if the outcome of one event does not affect the outcome of a second event. In the candy example, the probability of picking the lemon candy will always be 10% if a selected piece of candy is always placed back into the bag.

Here is another example of independent events: The set of genes inherited by one child does not affect the gene set inherited by a brother or sister. When two people with the sickle cell trait have children, every child has a 50% chance of inheriting one normal and one sickle cell beta globin gene, every child has a 25% chance of inheriting two normal beta globin genes, and every child has a 25% chance of inheriting two sickle cell beta globin genes.

outcomes are *AS, AS, SS,* and *SS.* Each child has a 50% chance of having the sickle cell trait (*AS*) and a 50% chance of having sickle cell anemia (*SS*).

The fixed pattern of sickle cell gene inheritance allows parents to predict how their genetic makeup may affect their children. The predictions help parents to decide whether to seek genetic testing of their infants.

6

DETECTING
SICKLE CELL ANEMIA

Ahuge global effort called the Human Genome Project had as its goal the identification of the nucleotide sequence of the 3 billion DNA bases in the human genome. The project started in October 1990, and by April 2003, scientists had sequenced a human genome. As a result of this sequencing, scientists now know that certain genes are found on certain chromosomes.

Chromosome 11 contains 1,300 to 1,900 genes. One of these genes encodes the beta globin protein of hemoglobin. The beta globin gene is found between base pair 5,203,272 and base pair 5,204,877. Scientists have identified nucleotide sequences in and near the beta globin gene. These data have helped researchers to develop DNA tests for the sickle cell gene.

DETECTING THE SICKLE CELL GENE WITH BACTERIAL ENZYMES

How can anyone tell the difference between a normal beta globin gene and the sickle cell beta globin gene? In theory, this should be easy. The genes differ in one crucial way: The sixth codon of sickle cell beta globin reads "GTG," instead of the normal "GAG." This means that a scientist could sequence a gene to see if it contains the critical "GTG" or "GAG." A doctor may want this type of test performed. However, DNA sequencing is time-consuming and costly. Another way to test DNA for the sickle cell gene requires special types of proteins made by bacteria.

Bacteria make proteins called **restriction enzymes**. These enzymes act like small scissors that cut DNA molecules. The enzymes do not cleave DNA at random places. Instead, a restriction enzyme seeks out a certain nucleotide sequence, which is called a **cleavage site**.

The restriction enzyme moves along the backbone of a DNA molecule until it comes across its cleavage site. Then, it binds to the DNA molecule. Once the enzyme is tightly bound to the DNA, it twists into a different shape. As the enzyme contorts, it kinks the DNA molecule and breaks the DNA backbone.

Different restriction enzymes attach to different cleavage sites. For example, a restriction enzyme called *Eco*RI seeks out the nucleotide sequence "GAATTC." *Eco*RI breaks a DNA molecule after the guanine (G) nucleotide in the cleavage site.

Scientists can use restriction enzymes to see whether two samples of DNA contain the same DNA molecules. This works because a change in nucleotide sequence can create or delete enzyme cleavage sites. A DNA analysis technique that uses restriction enzymes is called **restriction fragment length polymorphism** (**RFLP**). RFLP is quite a mouthful, but it has a simple meaning.

Human DNA has many cleavage sites for restriction enzymes. Depending upon the enzyme used, human DNA may be cleaved hundreds of thousands of times. Enzyme digestion produces DNA fragments.

Consider DNA from two people. Unless the people are identical twins, the nucleotide sequences of their DNA are going to be somewhat different. Some of these differences create cleavage sites for restriction enzymes, and some of these differences delete cleavage sites for restriction enzymes. Suppose that a restriction enzyme is used to digest samples of DNA from the two people. The enzyme cuts each DNA sample into DNA fragments of various lengths. Since the DNA samples contain different nucleotide sequences, the enzyme cuts the DNA samples into two different groups of DNA fragments.

"Polymorphism" means that something exists in different forms. A "length polymorphism" is something that exists in different lengths. So, RFLP refers to the ability of restriction enzymes to cleave nonidentical DNA samples into fragments that have different lengths.

A scientist performs the RFLP technique by digesting a DNA sample with a restriction enzyme to produce DNA fragments. DNA fragments are separated by size using electrophoresis. Digested DNA samples are placed in a gel slab. An electric current pulls the negatively charged DNA fragments through the gel and toward the positive electrode at the other end of the gel. The gel acts like a sieve. Smaller DNA fragments move through the gel faster than large DNA fragments.

Electrophoresis creates a pattern of DNA fragments that can look like a bar code. The RFLP pattern gives clues about the sample DNA. For example, the pattern can show whether two DNA samples are identical. Forensic scientists look for this type of information. An RFLP pattern can also show whether a DNA sample has a copy of a certain gene.

Using RFLP analysis, a researcher can decide if a human DNA sample contains the normal beta globin gene or the sickle cell beta globin gene. The single nucleotide mutation in the sickle cell gene changes the cleavage site for a variety of restriction enzymes. One of the enzymes is *Mst*II, which seeks the nucleotide sequence "CCTNAGG." The "N" in the *Mst*II cleavage site can be any of the four nucleotides (A, C, G, or T). In the gene that encodes normal beta globin, amino acids three to nine are encoded by the nucleotide sequence, CTG ACT CCT GAG GAG AAG TCT. This part of the beta globin gene has an *Mst*II cleavage site, where "N" is "G": CTGACTCCTGAGGAGAAGTCT.

The two DNA strands in this part of the normal beta globin gene can be pictured as follows:

. . . . CTGACTCCTGAGGAGAAGTCT. . . .
. . . . GACTGAGGACTCCTCTTCAGA. . . .

Notice that the bottom DNA strand also has an *Mst*II cleavage site (shown in red). Since it lies in the opposite DNA strand, the cleavage site reads in the opposite direction. Here, the "N" in the nucleotide sequence is "C."

The enzyme *Mst*II binds to its cleavage site in this area of the beta globin gene and cuts the DNA molecule after the "CC," as shown below:

. . . . CTGACTCC TGAGGAGAAGTCT . . . .
. . . . GACTGAGGACT CCTCTTCAGA . . . .

Examine the nucleotide sequences that encode amino acids three to nine of normal and sickle cell beta globins:

(normal gene)   CTGACTCCTGAGGAGAAGTCT
(sickle cell gene) CTGACTCCTGTGGAGAAGTCT

A mutation has changed the "GAG" of the normal human beta globin gene to the "GTG" of the sickle cell beta globin gene. As a result, the sickle cell gene loses the *Mst*II cleavage site. The enzyme does not cleave the sickle cell beta globin gene in this region.

*Mst*II cleaves the beta globin gene at a number of cleavage sites. If DNA containing the sickle cell gene is treated with *Mst*II, the enzyme produces a DNA fragment that has about 1,400 base pairs. This DNA fragment includes nucleotide sequences that encode amino acids three to nine of the beta globin gene.

*Mst*II treatment of the normal beta globin gene does not produce this large piece of DNA. The normal beta globin gene has the extra *Mst*II cleavage site. Instead of cutting DNA to produce a fragment of about 1,400 base pairs, *Mst*II cuts the DNA into two pieces of about 1,200 base pairs and 200 base pairs.

Think about this experiment. Focus on the two large DNA fragments. A fragment of 1,400 base pairs indicates the sickle cell gene and a fragment of 1,200 base pairs

NAME THAT CHROMOSOME

Fathers give their sons a Y chromosome. They also traditionally give their sons a family name. Examples of family names, or surnames, include Johnson, Sung, Abrams, Kitano, or Soto. Could there be a link between a surname and genetic markers in the Y chromosome? Men who have the same surname might have similar genetic markers.

United Kingdom scientists tested this theory. They compared Y chromosomal genetic markers from 150 pairs of men who share a British surname. The data revealed that sharing a surname increases the chance of sharing Y-chromosomal genetic markers. The link becomes strongest with rare surnames. That is, they found a clear link for a Widdowson or Attenborough, and no link for a Smith or Taylor.

indicates the normal gene. (1) What size of DNA fragment would appear after *Mst*II treatment of DNA from a person with normal beta globin genes? (2) What would be the result if DNA were obtained from a person who has sickle cell anemia? (3) How would this differ from the DNA of a person who has the sickle cell trait? The following results would be obtained:

(1) Normal beta globin genes only: a DNA fragment of 1,200 base pairs.
(2) Sickle cell anemia: a DNA fragment of 1,400 base pairs.
(3) Sickle cell trait: two types of DNA fragments (1,400 base pairs and 1,200 base pairs).

Scientists have devised various tests for the sickle cell gene using restriction enzymes. These tests can diagnose sickle cell anemia even before birth.

This discovery may assist police in their hunt for criminals. The researchers suggest that they would have to create a database of at least 40,000 surnames and Y chromosome data associated with those surnames. The database might help to focus a criminal investigation. After collecting crime scene DNA left by a male, a forensic scientist could analyze the Y chromosome for certain genetic markers. Comparing this information with the database might yield a number of surnames. Police could then compare the list of surnames against names on their list of suspects. This system would have limitations. Adoptions and name changes, for example, would sever links between surnames and Y chromosomal genetic markers. Still, such a database could offer one more tool for criminal investigators.

PRENATAL DIAGNOSIS: DETECTION OF THE SICKLE CELL GENE

A fetus does not make hemoglobin that contains any beta globin. In the fetus, the main form of hemoglobin—hemoglobin F—has two alpha globin proteins and two gamma globin proteins. Beta globin protein synthesis only becomes important starting around the time of birth. As a result, the presence of the sickle cell gene cannot be detected in a fetus by looking for sickle cell beta globin. The sickle cell gene itself must be detected with a DNA test.

Doctors use a number of techniques to obtain samples of fetal cells for DNA tests. One method is **amniocentesis**. In this test, a doctor inserts a hollow needle into the woman's uterus and takes a small amount of the fluid—the amniotic fluid—that surrounds the fetus. The fluid contains cells from the fetus.

A small number of fetal cells also travel through the mother's bloodstream. A new method takes advantage of this. Fetal cells are isolated from the mother's blood and the cells are purified for DNA testing.

These techniques yield only a small amount of DNA, which may be too small for RFLP analysis. Fortunately, bacteria make another type of useful enzyme: heat-resistant **DNA polymerase**.

A DNA polymerase is an enzyme that uses nucleotides to produce DNA. Certain bacteria have DNA polymerases that can resist high temperatures. These bacteria have to make tough enzymes because they live in very hot parts of the world with temperatures of about 212° Fahrenheit (100° Centigrade). One type of heat-resistant bacteria lives in a hot spring in Yellowstone National Park.

Scientists use heat-resistant DNA polymerase to make a huge number of copies of a selected nucleotide sequence

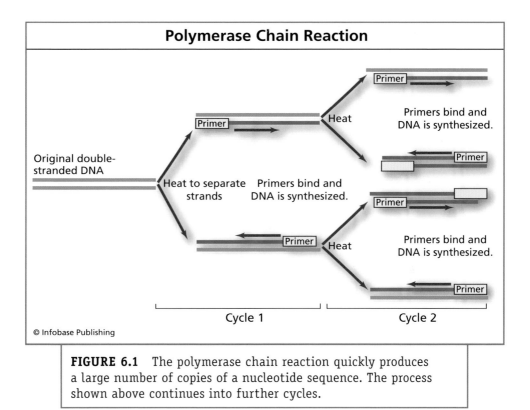

Polymerase Chain Reaction

Original double-stranded DNA

Heat to separate strands

Primers bind and DNA is synthesized.

Primer

Heat

Primer

Heat

Primers bind and DNA is synthesized.

Primer

Primers bind and DNA is synthesized.

Primer

Primer

Primer

Cycle 1

Cycle 2

© Infobase Publishing

FIGURE 6.1   The polymerase chain reaction quickly produces a large number of copies of a nucleotide sequence. The process shown above continues into further cycles.

with a process called the **polymerase chain reaction** (**PCR**). Before carrying out the PCR, the scientist must decide which nucleotide sequence to copy. The selected nucleotide sequence is sometimes called the target nucleotide sequence. The scientist makes two types of DNA molecules called **primers**. A primer is a single-stranded DNA molecule that has about 20 nucleotides. The primers have nucleotide sequences that allow them to bind with segments of DNA found at both ends of the target nucleotide sequence.

The first step in the polymerase chain reaction is heating a sample of DNA to separate the two strands of double-stranded DNA molecules. The sample is then cooled and the two types of primer added. Each primer binds to a DNA strand at one end of the target nucleotide sequence. Then, DNA polymerase synthesizes DNA by adding nucleotides to the primers.

How does the DNA polymerase add the correct nucleotides to copy DNA? The rules of base pairing determine the sequence. Recall that T pairs with an A, and G pairs with a C. An example of how a DNA polymerase can extend a primer by adding nucleotides is shown below. The DNA primer is shown in red and the new nucleotides in blue.

```
. . . . GCATGACAGGCCTAAGCTCG
. . . . CGTACTGTCCGGATTCGAGCGGACATAGCAATTCG. . . .
                          ↓
. . . . GCATGACAGGCCTAAGCTCGC
. . . . CGTACTGTCCGGATTCGAGCGGACATAGCAATTCG. . . .
                          ↓
. . . . GCATGACAGGCCTAAGCTCGCC
. . . . CGTACTGTCCGGATTCGAGCGGACATAGCAATTCG. . . .
                          ↓
. . . . GCATGACAGGCCTAAGCTCGCCT
. . . . CGTACTGTCCGGATTCGAGCGGACATAGCAATTCG. . . .
```

After completing DNA synthesis, the DNA sample is heated again to separate the DNA strands. Cooling the sample allows primers to bind with single-stranded DNA molecules. Another round of synthesis begins. By repeating these steps, a researcher can make a billion copies of the target nucleotide sequence in a few hours.

Since a researcher can make so many copies of a nucleotide sequence, only a very small amount of fetal DNA is needed to detect a sickle cell gene. Using PCR, a researcher makes millions of copies of a portion of the beta globin gene that includes the sixth codon. The copied DNA can then be treated with a restriction enzyme, such as *Mst*II. RFLP

RFLP AND PCR HELP CSIs

In 1986, police in the United Kingdom asked Dr. Alec Jeffreys for help in a criminal investigation. The police suspected that a teenage boy had killed two girls. They wanted Jeffreys to see if the boy's DNA matched a DNA sample found at a crime scene. Jeffreys used the new technique of restriction fragment length polymorphism (RFLP) to compare the DNA samples. They did not match.

The police hatched a new plan: They would use DNA tests to scare the killer from his hiding place. A call went out for blood samples from every male between the ages of 16 and 34 who lived near the crime scenes. The police collected samples from 5,000 men.

One DNA sample after the next failed to match the crime scene DNA. Then, a bakery manager told the police that a coworker had donated blood for a friend, a man named Colin Pitchfork who clearly did not want his own blood tested. The police arrested Pitchfork, and the man confessed. Later, DNA analysis verified that Colin Pitchfork's DNA matched the killer's DNA.

The RFLP method became the first scientifically accepted forensic DNA analysis technique in the United States. The large amount of DNA required for RFLP analysis caused a problem, however: Crime scenes do not always contain enough DNA. This is where the polymerase chain reaction (PCR) comes to the rescue. PCR can produce a billion copies of a target nucleotide sequence. To start producing copies with PCR, a forensic scientist needs only very small amounts of DNA. After making DNA copies, a forensic scientist can analyze the DNA using RFLP or other techniques.

Thanks to PCR, crime scene investigators can collect DNA evidence from a huge number of objects. DNA analysis can be performed with minute traces of biological samples collected from dental molds, cigarette butts, beverage cans, forks, spoons, chewing gum, ski masks, licked envelopes, toothbrushes, razor shavings, band-aids, clothing, and even fingerprints.

analysis can then reveal whether the sixth codon has the sickle cell mutation.

Detecting Sickle Cell Anemia After Birth

In the fetus, hemoglobin F has two alpha globin proteins and two gamma globin proteins. After birth, an infant starts to produce hemoglobin that has two alpha globin proteins and two beta globin proteins. If the infant has only normal beta globin genes, the infant makes Hemoglobin A. If the infant has a sickle cell beta globin gene, the infant makes Hemoglobin S. Now, a doctor can order a simple test to detect the presence of sickle cell hemoglobin in the blood of the infant.

What sort of test can distinguish between normal hemoglobin and sickle cell hemoglobin? Normal beta globin and sickle cell beta globin differ by a single amino acid. This amino acid change alters the overall charge of the beta globin. Various techniques can be used to detect whether beta globin has the charge characteristics of normal beta globin or sickle cell hemoglobin. One method is protein electrophoresis. Chromatography is also used to test for sickle cell hemoglobin. Both methods separate proteins by their different charges.

Large amounts of sickle cell hemoglobin and a lack of normal hemoglobin indicate sickle cell anemia. A mixture of normal and sickle cell hemoglobin suggests that the patient has the sickle cell trait. Methods for detecting sickle cell hemoglobin can be used in infants, children, and adults.

A doctor can also diagnose sickle cell anemia by symptoms. For example, sickle cell disease can cause a painful swelling of the hands and feet in infants and young children. In older children and adults, sickle cell anemia can cause pain in the head, chest, stomach, and back.

Doctors still use the classic test for sickle cell anemia, which is to look for sickled cells in the blood. A physician may choose to confirm a diagnosis for sickle cell anemia by examining a patient's DNA for the sickle cell beta globin gene.

7

CURRENT TREATMENTS FOR SICKLE CELL ANEMIA

Scientists know a great deal about sickle cell anemia. They know how a mutation in the beta globin gene causes many types of symptoms. They know how sickle cell anemia can be passed on from one generation to the next. But scientists do not yet know how to cure sickle cell anemia in all people who have the disease. Today, most treatments of sickle cell anemia aim to control symptoms and reduce complications of the disease.

DRUG TREATMENTS

Sickle cell anemia places a person at high risk for infections. This is especially true in children, in whom pneumonia is the leading cause of death. Doctors begin to treat sickle cell anemia soon after the birth of their sickle cell anemia patients.

In the United States, the District of Columbia and all 50 states test newborns for sickle cell disease. Typically, the test involves an examination of a very small blood sample for sickle cell hemoglobin. If sickle cell hemoglobin is detected, a doctor may confirm the result with a test for the sickle cell gene. An infant who has sickle cell anemia

GENETIC TESTS BEGIN TO ABOLISH A DISEASE

Tay-Sachs disease is a severe disorder of the nervous system caused by a defect in the synthesis of an enzyme. Normally, the enzyme breaks down certain fatty molecules. Without the enzyme, fatty molecules build up in brain nerve cells, distorting their shape and interfering with their function.

During the early years of life, a child with Tay-Sachs disease typically becomes blind and deaf, and finds it difficult to swallow. A child can also suffer paralysis and seizures. Often, devastating nervous system damage causes death by the age of five. Scientists have yet to find a useful treatment or a cure for the disease.

In the early 1970s, a method to test for Tay-Sachs disease in a fetus did not exist. The diagnosis could be made only after the infant was born. Five New York couples whose babies had Tay-Sachs disease decided to wipe out the disorder. They started a genetic testing program that focused on Ashkenazi Jews, whose ancestry could be traced back to communities in central and eastern Europe. Although the disease occurred in various populations, at that time, it had a high rate of occurrence among Ashkenazi Jews.

A massive education and genetic screening effort started around 1974. Volunteers educated people about genetic testing in Jewish community centers, synagogues, and colleges. They explained about tests that could identify people who carried one copy of the gene that causes Tay-Sachs disease. This disease, like sickle cell anemia, occurs when an infant inherits a copy of a disease-causing gene from each parent. Both parents must be carriers for the gene.

(continues)

(continued)

Some matchmakers advised men and women not to marry if both had the Tay-Sachs gene. Pregnant women who discovered that their fetus carried the disease often decided to terminate pregnancy.

After 30 years, the program began to abolish the disease. In the United States, the number of infants born with Tay-Sachs disease decreased from 50 per year to 5 per year. Of those 5, most are born to couples who are not Jewish. Today, most doctors have not seen a case of Tay-Sachs disease firsthand.

receives treatment at once. A doctor treats the young patient with penicillin, an antibiotic. The aim of the treatment is to prevent pneumonia. Studies have shown that early diagnosis and treatment reduces the risk of fatal illness in infants.

Throughout a person's life, sickle cell anemia can cause symptoms that require many types of drugs. For example, painkilling medicines treat pain from damaged, oxygen-starved tissues. A person may become dehydrated. If so, then a doctor may prescribe an intravenous infusion of fluids. Acute chest syndrome can cause a person to have trouble breathing. In this case, a doctor may treat the person with oxygen. Medicated creams may be used to treat leg ulcers.

The most unusual sickle cell anemia drug is a small molecule called hydroxyurea. The drug has a unique effect on hemoglobin production. In a person with sickle cell anemia, alpha globin pairs with sickle cell beta globin to form sickle cell hemoglobin. Hydroxyurea stimulates the synthesis of gamma globin. Now, alpha globin can pair with gamma globin to form fetal hemoglobin. Red blood cells contain fetal hemoglobin molecules and fewer sickle cell hemoglobin molecules. A decrease in the number of sickle cell hemoglobins decreases the formation of hemoglobin polymers, which means less sickling.

Adults who have sickle cell anemia can be treated with hydroxyurea to reduce the occurrence of severe pain and acute chest syndrome. But the drug has drawbacks. Not everyone responds to treatment. The drug may increase the risk of infections, decrease the function of bone marrow, and produce other toxic effects. So far, the drug has been approved to treat adults who have had severe complications. Hydroxyurea is not yet approved for children.

BLOOD TRANSFUSION

Another approach to treating sickle cell anemia is to decrease the number of red blood cells that can sickle. This can be achieved by diluting the number of unhealthy red blood cells by adding normal red blood cells. Another tactic is to swap sickled cells for healthy cells. Such treatments involve **blood transfusions**, the transfer of blood components from one person to another.

In sickle cell anemia, blood transfusion therapy increases the number of normal red blood cells. At the same time, the treatment decreases the number of cells that could transform to the sickle shape. A blood transfusion may be used to treat acute chest syndrome, severe anemia, and other complications. This treatment may also reduce the risk of stroke.

Doctors can choose among several methods to transfer red blood cells. Two methods are simple transfusion and red cell exchange transfusion. In a simple transfusion, red blood cells are removed from donated blood. The donated cells are infused into the vein of a patient. A doctor may select simple transfusion to rapidly boost the oxygen–carrying capacity of the patient's blood.

Repeated simple transfusions can cause the body to build up high concentrations of iron from old blood cells. Iron overload can damage the liver, heart, and other organs. To prevent this, a patient may have to take medicine to decrease dangerously high amounts of iron.

In a red cell exchange transfusion, red blood cells are swapped. A patient's red blood cells are removed and then replaced with normal red blood cells. This type of therapy helps to decrease the accumulation of iron associated with repeated simple transfusions.

BONE MARROW TRANSPLANT

Red blood cells are produced in the spongy tissues of bone marrow. In certain cases, doctors can cure sickle cell anemia by replacing the bone marrow of a person who has this disease with bone marrow that produces red cells with normal hemoglobin.

To transplant bone marrow, the patient's sickle cell–producing bone marrow must first be destroyed. This is achieved with toxic drugs or radiation. A sample of healthy bone marrow is removed from a donor. The patient then receives a transfusion of healthy bone marrow cells. The cells travel to the patient's bone marrow and begin production of red blood cells.

After the transplant, the patient gets drugs to prevent the body from rejecting the new bone marrow. Why would the patient's body reject the healthy bone marrow? The answer lies in the **immune system**, a group of organs that work together to defend the body against foreign invaders and poisonous substances. The body mounts defenses against bacteria, viruses, parasites, and toxins. Bone marrow, the spleen, tonsils, and other tissues produce and store **white blood cells**. White blood cells—the immune system's soldiers—hunt, attack, and digest invaders.

It is essential that white blood cells distinguish between cells that belong in the body and cells foreign to the body. How is this possible? Just as cattle carry the brand of their owner, a body's cells carry identification molecules. These markers can be found on the surface of human cells. A person's immune system attacks a cell that has surface markers that differ from those on the body's own cells. For example, the immune system detects the presence of foreign markers on bacteria, viruses, and parasites.

A molecule that rouses the immune system into attack mode is called an **antigen**. Certain white blood cells react

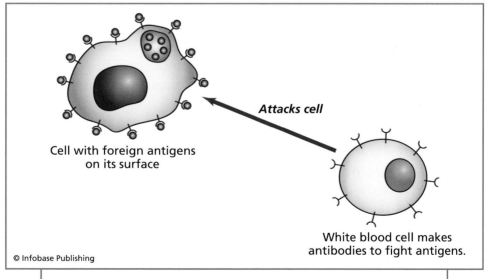

Attacks cell

Cell with foreign antigens
on its surface

White blood cell makes
antibodies to fight antigens.

© Infobase Publishing

FIGURE 7.1   A certain type of white blood cell attacks cells with foreign antigens.

to an antigen by attacking cells that have the antigen on their surface. Other white blood cells react to an antigen by making **antibodies**. An antibody is a protein that binds to an antigen and directs other white blood cells to attack it. Antibodies tag foreign cells for destruction.

The immune system destroys a bacterial cell because it has foreign antigens. What happens when a human cell from one person is injected into the body of another person? The immune system detects the new cell and may attack it because it is foreign.

Suppose that the bone marrow of a person with sickle cell anemia were replaced with healthy bone marrow from another person. Unless the transplanted bone marrow has the proper identification antigens, the immune system will attack the new tissue. The body is said to "reject" the new bone marrow. The risk of bone marrow rejection can be reduced by transplanting tissue with identification markers that match the patient's antigens as closely as possible. A patient's brother, sister, or parent may have suitable bone marrow. A person who is unrelated to the patient may also have bone marrow with suitable antigens. The chance that the patient's body will accept the donor bone marrow increases with the number of matching identification antigens.

White blood cells produced by the bone marrow are part of the immune system. After a bone marrow transplant, the new bone marrow can produce white blood cells that identify the other body tissues as foreign. The new white blood cells can attack the tissues of the patient. This is another reason why doctors try to match identification antigens between the donor's tissue and the patient's tissue.

While a bone marrow transplant offers a cure for some sickle cell anemia patients, the procedure itself can cause serious medical problems. Usually, doctors use this treatment

HELPING THE IMMUNE SYSTEM TO FIGHT INVADING MICROBES

When a disease-causing bacteria or virus enters the body, it triggers the body's defenses. If the immune system's cells have never encountered the invading microbe, then an effective response may require a week or more. This might be too slow to prevent illness. A **vaccine** helps the immune system to prepare for a bacteria or virus.

More than 200 years ago, an English country doctor named Edward Jenner made a crude type of vaccine. At that time, smallpox killed a million people in Europe every year. Most of the victims were children. Jenner noticed that milkmaids often became ill from a mild disease called cowpox. After they had cowpox, they did not catch fatal smallpox.

Jenner removed a small amount of fluid from the sores of Sarah Nelms, a young dairymaid who had cowpox. He injected the fluid into James Phipps, a healthy eight-year old. Weeks later, Jenner injected the boy with fluid from a smallpox sore. James Phipps did not become ill with the disease.

Scientists now know that viruses cause cowpox and smallpox. The viruses have similar antigens. When Jenner injected fluid with cowpox virus, he provoked an immune response against the antigens. The immune system learned how to deal with the virus. When Jenner injected fluid with smallpox virus, the immune system could mount a swift defense. The weaker cowpox virus served as a vaccine against the lethal smallpox virus.

In 1967, the World Health Organization launched a vaccination program to abolish smallpox. It worked. The year 1977 marked the last reported natural case of smallpox.

(continues)

(continued)

Scientists have made vaccines against more than 20 infectious diseases. Some vaccines contain weak or killed microbes. Others contain inactive toxins made by dangerous microbes. Other vaccines are made with new DNA technologies.

Vaccines number among the medicines used to treat infants with sickle cell anemia. In addition to antibiotics, infants receive vaccines that help their immune systems to recognize bacteria that cause pneumonia.

only for children who have a severe form of sickle cell anemia. Scientists are working on new treatments that may be safer and available to all who have sickle cell anemia.

8

POTENTIAL TREATMENTS FOR SICKLE CELL ANEMIA

Blood transfusions provide sickle cell anemia patients with an increased number of normal red blood cells and a decreased number of red blood cells that contain sickle cell hemoglobin. However, transfusions offer only short-term benefits because stem cells in the patient's bone marrow produce new red blood cells that carry sickle cell hemoglobin.

Since bone marrow cells are the source of the problem, one tactic is to kill the patient's bone marrow cells. The bone marrow is then replaced with tissue that can produce normal blood cells. This is the basis of bone marrow transplant therapy. Few qualify for a bone marrow transplant. One important limit of the therapy is that the transplanted cells must have identification antigens that match the patient's antigens as closely as possible. Otherwise, the patient's immune system will attack the new bone marrow tissue. Suitable donor bone marrow may be obtained from a patient's brother, sister, or parent, or even from a stranger.

In the late 1980s, doctors realized that human umbilical cord blood contains stem cells. Today, blood banks collect donated cord blood for stem cells. **Cord blood stem cells** have been used to treat over 40 diseases, including sickle

INHERITED DISEASE PROTECTS AGAINST BACTERIA

Cystic fibrosis (CF) is a severe genetic disease that causes the body to produce thick, sticky mucus. The mucus clogs organs of the body, including the lungs. Thick mucus makes it difficult to breathe and can allow the lungs to be infected with bacteria. The mucus can also block enzymes from entering the intestines, where they are needed to break down food for nutrients.

In the United States, about 30,000 people have CF. Although it occurs most often in Caucasians, anyone can inherit the genes that cause the disease. Like sickle cell anemia, CF occurs when a person inherits two copies of the mutant gene, one from each parent. The two diseases share another feature in that people who have one mutant gene and one normal gene have an advantage over those who have only normal genes.

cell anemia. This source of stem cells does not offer a treatment for everyone with sickle cell anemia. Antigens on cord blood stem cells must be matched as closely as possible to antigens on the patient's cells.

AN OVERVIEW OF GENE THERAPY

Another approach to treating sickle cell anemia involves **gene therapy**, a treatment in which the patient's own bone marrow cells are altered so that they contain normal beta globin genes. This tactic would be an improvement over blood transfusions because it offers a permanent solution. It would also avoid the dangerous immune responses that can occur with bone marrow transplants from another person.

A study suggests that the CF gene protects against typhoid fever, a life-threatening illness. A person gets typhoid fever by consuming food or water tainted with certain bacteria. Once inside the body, the microbes travel through the intestines and into the bloodstream. In the first step of this invasion, the bacteria must latch onto a protein found on the surface of intestinal cells. After binding the protein, the invaders pass through the cells and spread throughout the body. The CF gene encodes the protein that the typhoid microbes use to enter intestinal cells. A mutated CF gene does not produce the protein. Without the protein, microbes are locked out of the cells. Having one copy of a mutant CF gene offers some defense against infection. Having two copies, however, results in CF.

Gene therapy for sickle cell disease, however promising, has been difficult to achieve.

The goal of gene therapy is to treat an inherited disease by correcting defective genes. The treatment requires the following steps:

◆ Develop a delivery system that can carry a normal gene to cells that contain a defective gene.
◆ Deliver the normal gene to the target cells.
◆ Ensure that the normal gene functions as it should once inside the target cells.

In gene therapy, the gene that gets "transplanted" into the body cells is sometimes called a **transgene**. Cells that have been modified with a transgene are called **genetically modified cells**.

The first step of gene therapy requires a decision about a delivery system. What is the best way to deliver a therapeutic transgene to cells that have a defective gene? Many scientists choose modified viruses as their delivery system.

A virus is basically a nucleic acid molecule surrounded by a protein coat. Depending upon the virus, the nucleic acid molecule can be DNA or RNA. Outside of living cells, viruses cannot reproduce. They cannot make their own proteins or their own DNA or RNA. A virus makes copies of itself by hijacking the machinery of its host cell. The hijacking starts when a virus delivers its genetic material to a cell. The virus's genetic material instructs the cell to make the virus's proteins and nucleic acid molecules. Soon, new viruses begin to form in the cell.

Before a virus can serve as a delivery system in gene therapy, its nucleic acid must be altered. For example, a scientist may make at least two changes in the virus's nucleic acid molecule by adding the therapeutic transgene and by deleting nucleotide sequences that contain instructions for making copies of the virus. As a delivery system, the only function of the virus is to deliver the therapeutic transgene to the cells. Once inside the cells, the virus's nucleic acid molecule can insert the transgene into the cell's DNA.

On September 14, 1990, doctors performed the first gene therapy for an inherited disease. The disease was adenosine deaminase (ADA) deficiency. Children who have this disorder are born with two mutant copies of the ADA gene. The mutant genes produce nonfunctioning ADA enzymes that allow toxic chemicals to build up in the blood. These chemicals kill white blood cells, and, as a result, the body cannot protect itself against infections. The child can suffer repeated and severe infections, which can prove fatal.

One way to treat ADA deficiency is with a bone marrow transplant. New bone marrow with normal ADA genes produces white blood cells that make the ADA enzyme. Finding suitable bone marrow, however, poses a problem. The donor bone marrow must have antigens that closely match the patient's antigens.

Weekly injections of ADA enzyme provide another type of treatment. Enzyme therapy must continue for life. Although the treatment helps the patient's immune system, it is not a cure. The immune system remains weaker than normal.

ADA deficiency seemed like a good candidate for gene therapy. The genetic cause of the disease was known (a mutation in the ADA gene); the effect of the genetic mutation was known (lack of functional ADA enzyme); and the cell target was known (white blood cells).

In September 1990, doctors used gene therapy to treat Ashanthi DeSilva, a four-year-old girl who had ADA deficiency. They removed white blood cells from the girl and grew the cells in the lab. Then, they exposed the cells to modified virus DNA that contained a normal ADA gene. Viral DNA with the ADA gene became inserted in the cells' chromosomes. The doctors infused the genetically modified white blood cells into their patient. During the next several years, doctors repeated the gene therapy process about a dozen times. After a while, Ashanthi DeSilva's body produced about 25% of the normal amounts of ADA enzyme. The girl still needed injections of ADA enzyme, but at lower doses. Gene therapy did not completely cure the disease. Still, the treatment boosted Ashanthi's immune system and improved her health. She was able to attend school and experience a rather normal childhood.

Beta Globin Gene Therapy

Why have scientists yet to create a gene therapy for sickle cell anemia? It might seem that ADA deficiency and sickle cell anemia present similar challenges for gene therapy. After all, both diseases are caused by a mutation in one gene. The aims in treating the diseases, however, are very different.

In the treatment of ADA deficiency, the goal is to provide an enzyme that the body does not make. To treat sickle cell anemia, the aim is to provide normal beta globin in the correct cells, at the correct time, and at the correct dose.

 ◆ Normal beta globin must be made in developing red blood cells.
 ◆ The cells must make enough normal beta globin to bind with alpha globin. Normal beta globin and alpha globin form normal hemoglobin.
 ◆ If the cells also make sickle cell beta globin, then a competition occurs. Both types of beta globin compete to bind with alpha globin. To make normal hemoglobin, normal beta globin must outcompete sickle cell beta globin.

Designing gene therapy for sickle cell anemia has proved a challenge for more than ten years. One approach to treating sickle cell anemia with gene therapy is as follows:

1. Bone marrow stem cells are obtained from the patient.
2. The cells are cultured—that is, the cells are grown in sterile, plastic containers with a liquid that provides nutrients.
3. A modified virus is added to the cells. The virus enters the cells and releases its nucleic acid molecule, which includes a normal beta globin gene. The beta globin gene inserts into the cell's DNA.

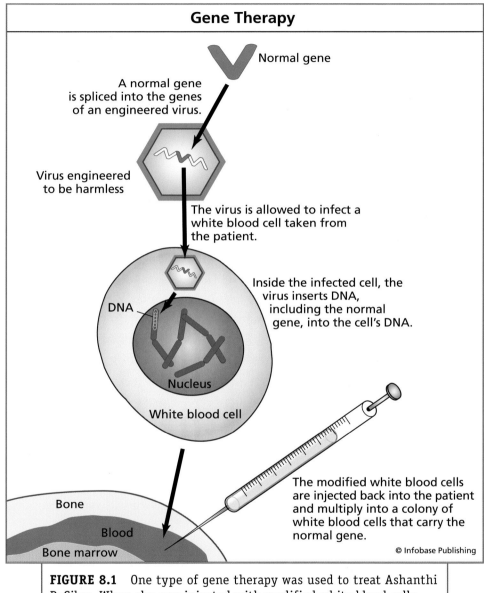

Gene Therapy

Normal gene

A normal gene is spliced into the genes of an engineered virus.

Virus engineered to be harmless

The virus is allowed to infect a white blood cell taken from the patient.

DNA

Inside the infected cell, the virus inserts DNA, including the normal gene, into the cell's DNA.

Nucleus

White blood cell

The modified white blood cells are injected back into the patient and multiply into a colony of white blood cells that carry the normal gene.

Bone

Blood

Bone marrow

© Infobase Publishing

FIGURE 8.1 One type of gene therapy was used to treat Ashanthi DeSilva. When she was injected with modified white blood cells, the new genes allowed her body to begin making ADA.

The genetically modified cell begins to make normal beta globin.

4. The genetically modified cells are returned to the patient.

Scientists have used this approach in mice that have a sickle cell disease. They removed a sample of bone marrow from the mice and isolated stem cells. Then, they added the beta globin gene to the stem cells. The scientists treated mice with radiation to kill bone marrow cells and then transplanted the genetically modified cells. After the transplant, the mice produced normal red blood cells.

The contest between normal and sickle cell beta globins presents a serious problem. Cells taken from a person with sickle cell anemia make sickle cell beta globin. When a gene for normal beta globin is added, the normal beta globin must compete with sickle cell beta globin for alpha globin. Scientists have devised ways to ensure that sickle cell beta globin loses this contest. One approach has been to create modified beta globin genes that have a greater attraction for alpha globin than normal beta globin. The genes encode an altered type of beta globin that functions as beta globin should. This increased attraction helps the modified beta globin to outcompete sickle cell beta globin. Another approach has been to genetically modify cells to produce gamma globin. Compared with normal beta globin, gamma globin has a greater attraction for alpha globin.

Before trying sickle cell anemia gene therapy in a human, scientists must solve another problem. When viruses deliver a transgene that inserts into human DNA, the transgene inserts in a random place. This can have serious consequences. For example, the transgene may insert into a gene vital to the cell's survival. Studies suggest that gene therapy with certain viruses may cause cancer. Trading sickle cell anemia for cancer is not a good therapy.

Ideally, gene therapy should allow a swap in the cell's DNA in which a normal beta globin gene is exchanged for a sickle cell beta globin gene. Such a swap is possible using a certain type of stem cell.

THERAPY WITH GENETICALLY MODIFIED STEM CELLS

During 2006, two research groups reported studies with mice using a new type of gene therapy for sickle cell anemia. The new gene therapy has two key features:

◆ Stem cells are used that make the same antigens produced by the patient's cells. These stem cells should not provoke an immune reaction in the patient.

◆ The stem cells are treated to replace sickle cell beta globin genes with normal beta globin genes. This replacement avoids the random insertion of a transgene that occurs with virus gene therapy.

To see how such a therapy is possible, it is time to take a closer look at stem cells.

Typically, a cell that has developed special functions cannot transform into a different type of cell. For example, a white blood cell cannot develop into a brain cell. Certain cells, such as stem cells, can transform into different types of cells. Bone marrow stem cells, for instance, can develop into red blood cells, white blood cells, and other components of blood.

Stem cells can be divided into two categories: embryonic stem cells and nonembryonic stem cells. In other words, some stem cells come from embryos, and some come from other sources. Generally, stem cells from embryos can transform into more types of cells than nonembryonic stem

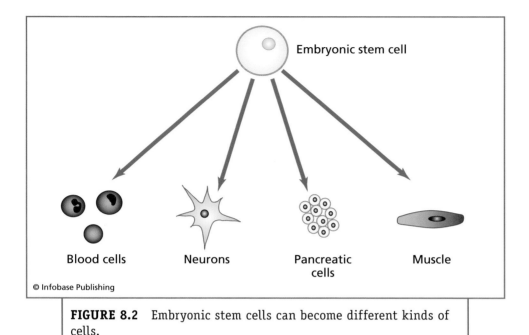

FIGURE 8.2 Embryonic stem cells can become different kinds of cells.

cells. Stem cells obtained from a very early embryo can develop into many types of body cells.

In a lab, a scientist can treat embryonic stem cells so that the cells develop into bone marrow stem cells. Suppose that this was performed with embryonic stem cells that had normal beta globin genes and no sickle cell genes. What might happen if the new bone marrow stem cells were used to treat a person with sickle cell anemia? The chances are that the new stem cells would have antigens that differ from the patient's antigens. As a result, the patient's immune system would attack the new cells.

Scientists have devised a technique that may solve the immune system problem. It is called **somatic cell nuclear transfer** (SCNT). A **somatic cell** is any cell other than a sperm cell or egg cell. A skin cell is an example of a somatic cell. The technique requires the transfer of the nucleus from a somatic cell into another cell.

It works like this: A scientist uses a very thin needle to remove the nucleus from an egg cell and the nucleus from a somatic cell—usually a skin cell. The scientist then injects the somatic cell nucleus into the egg cell. In a laboratory, the egg cell develops into a very young embryo. The scientist removes embryonic stem cells from the embryo.

Suppose that a scientist uses the SCNT technique with a skin cell from a person who has sickle cell anemia. The skin cell's nucleus is transferred to an egg cell that lacks a nucleus. The egg cell develops into a young embryo. Stem cells from the embryo are treated to make them develop into bone marrow stem cells. The bone marrow stem cells contain the patient's genetic information and make the patient's identification antigens. When transplanted into the patient, the new bone marrow stem cells should not provoke the immune system to attack.

The SCNT method would solve the immune system problem. But there is another problem to solve. The new bone marrow stem cells still carry the patient's genetic information, including the sickle cell genes. The solution is to swap out the sickle cell genes with normal beta globin genes before transplanting the bone marrow stem cells. This is possible thanks to **DNA crossover**.

DNA crossover is a process in which bits of DNA are exchanged between two DNA molecules. The exchange can occur when two DNA molecules line up together and the bits of DNA contain two areas of identical nucleotide sequences. The cell uses the stretches of identical nucleotide sequences like handles to swap pieces of DNA. Any nucleotide sequences that lie between these handles get moved as well.

In sickle cell gene therapy, a scientist can use a DNA crossover to eliminate sickle cell genes and introduce normal ones. Suppose that cells grown in a laboratory have DNA that contains the sickle cell beta globin gene.

The gene and nearby nucleotide sequences might appear as follows:

. . . . TGCAGTACTTAA-| Sickle cell |-GTCCATGCCTA. . . .
. . . . ACGTCATGAATT-|beta globin gene|-CAGGTACGGAT. . . .

To swap out the sickle cell gene, a scientist can create a DNA molecule, called **vector DNA**, which delivers a normal beta globin gene. To promote DNA crossover, the vector DNA contains a normal beta globin gene flanked by the same nucleotide sequences that flank the sickle cell beta globin gene in the cell's DNA.

. . . . TGCAGTACTTAA-| Normal |-GTCCATGCCTA. . . .
. . . . ACGTCATGAATT-|beta globin gene|-CAGGTACGGAT. . . .

The scientist then exposes the cells to the vector DNA. Using the nucleotide sequences that flank the beta globin genes, DNA crossover exchanges the cell's sickle cell beta globin gene with a normal beta globin gene. After DNA crossover, the cell has normal beta globin genes, and the vector DNA molecules have sickle cell beta globin genes. As the cells divide, vector DNA molecules are destroyed.

Here is how these techniques fit together to form a possible treatment for sickle cell anemia.

- ◆ Remove the nucleus from an egg cell.
- ◆ Remove the nucleus from a skin cell of the patient.
- ◆ Transfer the skin cell nucleus into the egg cell.
- ◆ Allow the egg cell to develop into a young embryo.
- ◆ Remove embryonic stem cells from the young embryo.
- ◆ Grow the embryonic stem cells in a laboratory.

- ◆ Use DNA crossover to swap the sickle cell genes in the stem cells with normal beta globin genes.
- ◆ Treat the genetically modified embryonic stem cells so that they develop into genetically modified bone marrow stem cells.
- ◆ Treat the patient to kill bone marrow cells that produce red blood cells with sickle cell hemoglobin.
- ◆ Transplant genetically modified bone marrow stem cells into the patient.
- ◆ The genetically modified bone marrow stem cells produce the patient's identification antigens and normal beta globin.

Scientists have proposed that this complex treatment might offer a cure for sickle cell anemia. As of mid-2007, the treatment was a proposal only. Scientists have performed steps of the treatment in mice, but treating humans is controversial.

9

SICKLE CELL ANEMIA: A HISTORY OF ETHICAL CONCERNS

In the 1940s, scientists labeled sickle cell anemia as the first "molecular disease." The production of an abnormal molecule could be linked to disease symptoms. Soon, researchers learned more details about sickle cell hemoglobin and how it distorted red blood cells. Research progressed, but a cure failed to appear. By the early 1970s, sickle cell anemia was called "the neglected disease."

In 1972, President Richard Nixon signed into law the Sickle Cell Anemia Control Act. The law aimed to reduce death from sickle cell anemia and promote research into new treatments. The law was intended to increase awareness about the disease. However, new sickle cell anemia screening programs created controversies. The majority of those tested were school-aged children and young adults. The purpose of the screening program remained unclear. By the time that anyone with sickle cell anemia reached school age, a doctor would have detected the disease by observing a patient's symptoms.

The focus of many early screening programs also proved to be a problem. The testing was aimed almost entirely at African Americans, but people of Mediterranean origins and others have sickle cell anemia. For that matter, anyone who inherits two copies of the sickle cell gene will have sickle cell anemia. Another problem with the tests was that officials at some local and state testing centers confused sickle cell anemia with sickle cell trait. A person with one sickle cell gene and one normal gene has the sickle cell trait, not sickle cell anemia. Many African Americans who had the sickle cell trait were denied health insurance and job prospects based on testing.

In time, medical studies helped to educate the public about the difference between sickle cell anemia and sickle cell trait. Legislators passed laws that required genetic test results to be treated as private information.

Government-sponsored testing of sickle cell anemia gained a valid purpose in the 1980s. The testing of infants saved lives. If a doctor found that a newborn had sickle cell anemia, then antibiotic treatment could begin right away. Treatment with antibiotics and vaccines put a stop to fatal infections.

In 2004, the U.S. Postal Service issued a stamp to highlight sickle cell disease. Stamp designer James Gurney created an image of a mother holding her baby. The design, which includes the inscription, "Test Early for Sickle Cell," conveys the importance of early testing.

GENE THERAPY TRIALS AND ERRORS

New therapies for sickle cell anemia have also sparked disputes. During the early 1970s, a chemical called urea was thought to be a cure. In one very small study, urea appeared to restore a patient's sickled cells to the normal shape. Later studies failed to show this helpful effect. By 1974, scientists found that urea not only failed to offer a cure but was toxic.

In the 1980s, scientists became overly eager about gene therapy. At the end of the decade, some promised that gene therapy for sickle cell anemia was in reach. Yet no therapy appeared. At a 1997 science meeting, a researcher announced that nobody had a gene therapy system that produced enough hemoglobin to treat sickle cell anemia. He concluded that gene therapy for sickle cell anemia seemed unlikely.

Progress for gene therapies has been more like a roller-coaster ride than a slow, constant climb. Doctors achieved positive results in the 1990 gene therapy trial to treat ADA deficiency. Eager researchers performed over 400 clinical gene therapy tests worldwide to treat various diseases, yet very few worked.

The field of gene therapy faced disaster when a patient died while participating in a gene therapy trial in 1999. Investigations by the federal government revealed that researchers had failed to follow rules about reporting poor results in gene therapy trials. Some claimed that at least six unreported deaths had occurred following genetic treatments. Since that time, the government has increased inspections

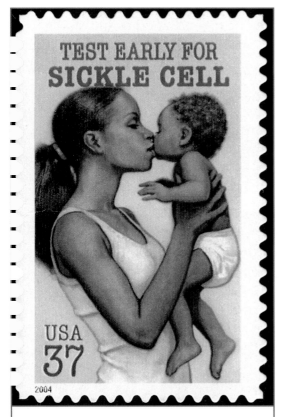

FIGURE 9.1   This Sickle Cell Disease Awareness commemorative stamp was released by the United States Postal Service in 2004. Its message was intended to emphasize the importance of sickle cell trait testing and to raise support for research into finding a cure.

NEGLECTED AT ONE TIME

During 1970, Dr. Robert B. Scott wrote about the neglect of sickle cell anemia. In Scott's view, the public failed to recognize the need for finding ways to treat the disease. Other diseases had captured the public's attention.

In 1967, doctors reported 1,155 new cases of sickle cell anemia. During the same year, doctors saw 813 new cases of the disease called muscular dystrophy. Yet groups raised $7.9 million for muscular dystrophy and less than $100,000 for sickle cell anemia.

Scott said that many local groups were working to control sickle cell anemia. He suggested that these efforts needed to be organized at a national level. Today, the United States has well-known organizations devoted to helping those with sickle cell anemia. The Sickle Cell Disease Association of America, Inc. (SCDAA), for example, supports member groups across the country.

of gene therapy trials. Not surprisingly, public participation in gene therapy trials decreased.

Researchers continue to pursue gene therapy even though it has proved much more difficult than many first thought. For example, viruses seemed to offer a good way to deliver a therapeutic gene. The problem with viral DNA is that it can insert itself at a random position in a cell's DNA. In 2003, scientists reported that two children developed cancer after receiving cells treated with viral DNA gene therapy. The viral DNA had become inserted in a way that promoted the growth of cancer cells.

In 2006, scientists suggested a sickle cell anemia gene therapy that avoided the viral DNA problem. The proposed therapy requires somatic cell nuclear transfer (SCNT) to produce stem cells.

DISPUTES ABOUT STEM CELL THERAPIES

Scientists have used the SCNT method with mice and other animals. In 2004, scientists at Seoul National University in South Korea announced the first use of SCNT to create human embryonic stem cells. During January 2006, university investigators reported their conclusion that the researchers had faked the data.

It is unclear whether SCNT can be used to produce human embryonic stem cells. Even if this can be done, people argue that it should not be done. In fact, at least six states have laws that ban the use of SCNT with human cells.

One reason why some people do not want the SCNT technique to be used with human cells concerns cloning. In theory, a **clone** is a copy of another life form. Scientists have used the SCNT method to produce clones of mice, sheep, and other animals. Could the SCNT process create a human clone? Nobody knows, but many do not want to find out.

The cloning objection does not seem to present a real barrier to SCNT. The purpose of using the SCNT method to treat a disease is very distinct from using the method to make a human clone. A second reason for objecting to SCNT revolves around the question of when a human life begins. Some people argue that the SCNT method should not be used with human cells. The reasoning is that the method requires the creation and destruction of an early embryo. This should not be allowed, the argument goes, because these very young embryos have the status of a human being. As such, the embryos should not be destroyed. Others argue that these early embryos are a mass of cells that lack

BRING IN THE CLONES

In 1997, scientists in Scotland announced the birth of Dolly, the first reproductively cloned animal. To clone a sheep, the scientists used a type of somatic cell nuclear transfer (SCNT). After removing the nucleus from a sheep egg cell, they fused the cell with a somatic cell taken from another sheep. Fusion produced an egg cell with a full set of chromosomes. The fused cell developed into a young embryo, which the scientists transferred to the womb of a third sheep. This new mother sheep gave birth to Dolly.

Scientists have used SCNT to clone cattle and pigs as well as sheep. Interest in cloning is not limited to livestock. Researchers have been trying to clone wild animals that face extinction. A rare antelope, a tiger, and the giant panda are species that have been proposed for cloning.

Cloning may offer a way to rescue endangered species. However, much research must be performed to develop efficient SCNT methods that ensure the success of producing a healthy clone.

---

human status. Is it ethical, they ask, to disregard a technique that may be used to cure diseases?

Further research will answer the question about whether SCNT can provide human embryonic stem cells. Science alone, however, will not answer the question about whether the technique *should* be used this way.

A SIMPLE DISEASE WITHOUT A SIMPLE CURE

About one century ago, James Herrick described sickle cell anemia for the first time in a Western medical journal.

Scientists later showed that the disease had a simple cause: a mutation of one nucleotide in the beta globin gene. Devising a cure for sickle cell anemia has not been simple. It may require a combination of gene therapy and stem cell therapy, two techniques that challenge scientific knowledge and raise ethical questions. In the meantime, doctors and researchers continue to learn about the disease and develop treatments to help those with sickle cell anemia manage their symptoms.

GLOSSARY

alpha globin   A protein that can pair with normal beta globin protein to form normal hemoglobin, with mutant beta globin to form sickle cell hemoglobin, or with gamma globin to form fetal hemoglobin.

amino acid   The chemical building block of protein.

amniocentesis   A prenatal test that requires a sample of the amniotic fluid that surrounds a fetus.

anemia   A condition in which there are too few red blood cells or the red blood cells do not function normally.

antibody   A protein that binds with a substance foreign to a body.

antigen   A substance that the immune system recognizes as foreign.

artery   A thick-walled blood vessel that carries blood away from the heart.

base   A nitrogen-containing molecule that forms part of DNA and RNA.

base pair   Two specific bases, held together by weak bonds, in nucleic acids; adenine (A) pairs with thymine (T), and cytosine (C) pairs with guanine (G).

beta globin   A protein that pairs with alpha globin to form hemoglobin.

biconcave   The condition of having two surfaces that curve inward.

blood transfusion   The transfer of blood components from one person to another.

bone marrow   Bone cavity tissue that produces blood cells.

capillary   A very thin-walled blood vessel that connects small arteries to small veins.

chromatin   A mixture of proteins, DNA, and RNA.

chromatography   A method of separating chemicals by their properties.

chromosome   A structure in a cell nucleus that contains genes.

cleavage site   A target nucleotide sequence for a restriction enzyme.

clone   A copy of a life form.

codon   A group of three nucleotides that code for an amino acid.

cord blood stem cells   Stem cells in the blood of an umbilical cord.

cytoplasm   A cell's cytosol and organelles found outside the nucleus.

cytosol   A mixture of water, salts, and proteins that surround a cell's organelles.

daughter cell   One of the cells formed by cell division.

deoxyribonucleic acid (DNA)   A nucleic acid molecule that encodes genetic information and contains deoxyribose sugar.

DNA crossover   A process in which two DNA molecules swap pieces of DNA.

DNA polymerase   An enzyme that uses nucleotides to make DNA.

electrophoresis   The use of an electric current to separate molecules.

endoplasmic reticulum   A system of folded membranes in a cell; site of protein synthesis.

gamete   An egg cell or a sperm cell.

gene   A nucleotide sequence that encodes a protein.

gene therapy   A treatment of a genetic disorder that aims to replace or supplement an abnormal gene with a normal gene.

genetic code   A sequence of nucleotide triplets that determines the sequence of amino acids in a protein.

genetic marker   A gene or piece of DNA with an identifiable location on a chromosome, the inheritance of which can be tracked.

genetically modified cell   A cell altered by manipulation of its DNA.

genome   The complete nucleotide sequences of an individual or species.

globin   A type of globular protein found in hemoglobin.

heme group   An iron-containing molecule found in hemoglobin.

hemoglobin   A heme group-containing protein that transports oxygen.

hemoglobin A (Hb A)   Hemoglobin composed of two alpha globins and two beta globins, normally produced by children and adults.

hemoglobin F (Hb F)   Hemoglobin composed of two alpha globins and two gamma globins, normally produced by a fetus.

hemoglobin S (Hb S)   Hemoglobin composed of two alpha globins and two sickle cell beta globins, produced by a person who has a sickle cell gene.

hypoxia   An insufficient supply of oxygen in the body.

immune system   A group of organs and cells that defend the body against microbes, toxins, and foreign materials.

meiosis   A type of cell division required to produce egg cells and sperm cells, which contain only half the normal number of chromosomes.

messenger RNA   An RNA molecule that carries the genetic information from the DNA in the nucleus to the protein-making apparatus of the cell.

mitochondria   Organelles that function as a cell's power plant.

mitosis   A type of cell division that produces two daughter cells that are identical to the parent cell and to each other.

monomer   A simple molecule that can combine with similar or identical molecules to form a polymer.

mutation   A change in the nucleotide sequence of a DNA molecule or a change in the amino acid sequence of a protein.

nucleotide   The basic unit of DNA, containing a sugar molecule, a chemical group that contains phosphorus, and a nitrogen-containing base.

nucleus   The organelle that contains most of a cell's DNA.

organelle   A membrane-bound structure that performs a function within a cell.

peptide   A chain of amino acids that is smaller than a protein.

plasma   A clear, yellow fluid that remains after all cells are removed from blood.

pluripotential stem cell   A cell that can develop into many types of specialized cells.

pneumonia   A disorder of the lungs, often caused by a bacterial or viral infection.

polymer   A large chemical made by combining smaller units.

polymerase chain reaction (PCR)   A process that produces millions of copies of a short nucleotide sequence.

primer   A small, single-stranded DNA molecule used to begin DNA synthesis in the polymerase chain reaction.

protein   A polymer of amino acids.

restriction enzyme   A protein that cleaves a DNA molecule at or near a certain nucleotide sequence.

restriction fragment length polymorphism (RFLP)   Variation between individuals in the pattern of DNA fragments obtained by treating DNA with a restriction enzyme.

reticulocyte   An immature red blood cell.

ribonucleic acid (RNA)   A nucleic acid molecule that can encode genetic information and contains ribose sugar.

sickle cell anemia   A disease resulting from the inheritance of a sickle cell beta globin gene from both parents.

sickle cell disease   A disorder resulting from the inheritance of two abnormal beta globin genes—one from each parent—in which one gene is the sickle cell beta globin gene.

sickle cell trait   A non-disease condition resulting from the inheritance of a sickle cell beta globin gene from one parent and a normal beta globin gene from the other parent.

somatic cell   A cell other than an egg cell or a sperm cell.

somatic cell nuclear transfer (SCNT)   The transfer of a nucleus from a somatic cell into an egg cell that lacks a nucleus.

stroke   An abrupt decrease of blood flow to the brain.

thalassemia   A disease caused by impaired hemoglobin protein synthesis.

transcription   The process in which the genetic information in DNA is copied into an RNA molecule.

transgene   A gene that is transferred to a cell; for example, in gene therapy.

translation   The process in which the information in the nucleotide sequence of messenger RNA is used to synthesize protein.

vaccine   A material that stimulates the immune system.

vaso-occlusion   The blockage of blood vessels.

vector DNA   A DNA molecule that can be used to deliver a transgene.

vein   A blood vessel that carries blood toward the heart.

white blood cell   A cell of the immune system that attacks foreign bacteria and viruses.

BIBLIOGRAPHY

Allison, Anthony C. "Two Lessons from the Interface of Genetics and Medicine." *Genetics* 166 (2004): 1591–1599.

Anderson, Nina. "Hydroxyurea Therapy: Improving the Lives of Patients with Sickle Cell Disease." *Pediatric Nursing* 32 (2006): 541–543.

"A Science Primer," National Center for Biotechnology Information Web Site. Available online. URL: http://www.ncbi.nlm.nih.gov/About/primer/genetics_cell.html.

Ashley-Koch, A., Q. Yang, and R.S. Olney. "Sickle Hemoglobin (Hb S) Allele and Sickle Cell Disease: A HuGE Review." *American Journal of Epidemiology* 151 (2000): 839–845.

Battey, James F. Jr., and Laura K. Cole. "A Stem Cell Primer." *Pediatric Research* 59 (2006): 1R–3R.

Bender, M.A. "Sickle Cell Disease," Gene Tests Web Site. Available online. URL: http://www.genetests.org/.

Benz, Edward J. "Hemoglobinopathies." In *Harrison's Principles of Internal Medicine,* 16th ed., edited by Dennis L. Kasper, Eugene Braunwald, Anthony S. Fauci, Stephen L. Hauser, Dan L. Longo, and J. Larry Jameson, 593–601. New York: The McGraw-Hill Companies, Inc., 2005.

Bojanowski, Jennifer. "Sickle Cell Disease," Health A to Z Web Site. Available online. URL: http://www.healthatoz.com/healthatoz/Atoz/common/standard/transform.jsp?requestURI=/healthatoz/Atoz/ency/sickle_cell_disease.jsp.

"Bone Marrow Transplantation and Peripheral Blood Stem Cell Transplantation: Questions and Answers," National Cancer Institute Web Site. Available online. URL: http://

www.cancer.gov/cancertopics/factsheet/Therapy/ bone-marrow-transplant.

Bridges, Kenneth R. "Sickle Cell Disease," Information Center for Sickle Cell and Thalassemic Disorders Web site. Available online. URL: http://sickle.bwh.harvard.edu/menu_ sickle.html.

Buchanan, George R., Michael R. DeBaun, Charles T. Quinn, and Martin H. Steinberg. "Sickle Cell Disease." *Hematology* (2004): 35–47.

Casey, Denise. "Primer on Molecular Genetics," Human Genome Project Web Site. Available online. URL: http://www. ornl.gov/sci/techresources/Human_Genome/publicat/ primer/toc.html.

Chang, Judy C., Lin Ye, and Yuet Wai Kan. "Correction of the Sickle Cell Mutation in Embryonic Stem Cells." *Proceedings of the National Academy of Sciences* 103 (2006): 1036–1040.

Clark, Melody S., Andrew Clarke, Charles S. Cockell, Peter Convey, H. William Detrich III, Keiron P.P. Fraser, Ian A. Johnston et al. "Antarctic Genomics." *Comparative and Functional Genomics* 5 (2004): 230–238.

Cook, Jerome E., and Jerome Meyer. "Severe Anemia with Remarkable Elongated and Sickle-shaped Red Blood Cells and Chronic Leg Ulcer." *Archives of Internal Medicine* 16 (1915): 644–651.

Cromie, William J. "Cystic Fibrosis Gene Found to Protect Against Typhoid," The Harvard University Gazette Web Site. Available online. URL: http://www.hno.harvard.edu/ gazette/1998/07.09/CysticFibrosisG.html.

Devlin, Thomas M., ed. *Textbook of Biochemistry with Clinical Correlations,* 4th ed. New York: Wiley-Liss, 1997.

Distenfeld, Ariel, and Ulrich Woermann. "Sickle Cell Anemia," eMedicine Web Site. Available online. URL: http://www. emedicine.com/MED/topic2126.htm.

Drayna, Dennis. "Founder Mutations." *Scientific American* 293 (2005): 78–85.

Emmel, Victor E. "A Study of the Erythrocytes in a Case of Severe Anemia with Elongated and Sickle-shaped Red Blood Corpuscles." *Archives of Internal Medicine* 20 (1917): 586–598.

Feldman, Simon D., and Alfred I. Tauber. "Sickle Cell Anemia: Reexamining the First 'Molecular Disease.'" *Bulletin of the History of Medicine* 71 (1997): 623–650.

"Genes on the Go: Charting the History of Human Migration." *Today's Science on File* 13 (2005): 270–272.

Goodman, S.R. "Preface: Thematic Issue on Sickle Cell Disease." *Cellular and Molecular Biology* 50 (2004): 1–4.

Griffiths, Anthony J.F., Jeffrey H. Miller, David T. Suzuki, Richard C. Lewontin, and William M. Gelbart. *An Introduction to Genetic Analysis,* 5th ed. New York: W.H. Freeman and Company, 1993.

Hamosh, Ada, Victor A. McKusick, Paul Brennan, Gary A. Bellus, and Cassandra L. Kniffin. "Sickle Cell Anemia," Online Mendelian Inheritance in Man Web Site. Available online. URL: http://www.ncbi.nlm.nih.gov/entrez/query. fcgi?cmd=Retrieve&db=OMIM&dopt=Detailed&tmpl= dispomimTemplate&list_uids=603903.

Herrick, James B. "Peculiar Elongated and Sickle-shaped Red Blood Corpuscles in a Case of Severe Anemia." *Archives of Internal Medicine* 6 (1910): 517–521.

Hicks, Nancy. "Doctor Asks Curb of Negro Disease." *New York Times*, October 27, 1970.

Hicks, Nancy. "Sickle Cell Trait Found in Athletes." *New York Times*, August 21, 1973.

Hoffbrand, Victor, Paul Moss, and John Pettit. *Essential Haematology,* 5th ed. Oxford, UK: Blackwell Publishing Ltd., 2006.

Ingram, V.M. "Gene Mutations in Human Hæmoglobin: The Chemical Difference Between Normal and Sickle Cell Hæmoglobin." *Nature* 180 (1957): 326–328.

Ingram, Vernon M. "Sickle-Cell Anemia Hemoglobin: The Molecular Biology of the First 'Molecular Disease'—the Crucial Importance of Serendipity." *Genetics* 167 (2004): 1–7.

Jenkins, Mark A., and Caryn Honig. "High Altitude and Athletic Training," SportsMed Web Site. Available online. URL: http://www.rice.edu/~jenky/sports/altitude.html.

Jones, P. "Oxygen Therapeutics Flow Through Product Pipelines of North American Companies." Что Нового: в науке и технике (*What's New: in Science and Technology*) 11 (2003): 54–60.

Kaye, Celia I. "Newborn Screening Fact Sheets." *Pediatrics* 118 (2006): e934–e963.

Kenner, Carole, Agatha M. Gallo, and Kellie D. Bryant. "Promoting Children's Health Through Understanding of Genetics and Genomics." *Journal of Nursing Scholarship* 37 (2005): 308–314.

King, Turi E., Stéphane J. Ballereau, Kevin E. Schürer, and Mark A. Jobling. "Genetic Signatures of Coancestry Within Surnames." *Current Biology* 16 (2006): 384–388.

Kolata G. "Using Genetic Tests, Ashkenazi Jews Vanquish a Disease." *New York Times*, February 18, 2003.

Krishnamurti, L. "Hematopoietic Cell Transplantation for Sickle Cell Disease: State of the Art." *Expert Opinion on Biological Therapy* 7 (2007): 161–172.

Lanza, Robert P., Betsy L. Dresser, and Philip Damiani. "Cloning Noah's Ark." *Scientific American* 283 (2000): 84–89.

"Learning About Sickle Cell Disease," National Institutes of Health Web site. Available online. URL: http://www.genome.gov/10001219.

Lonergan, Gael J., David B. Cline, and Susan L. Abbondanzo. "Sickle Cell Anemia." *RadioGraphics* 21 (2001): 971–994.

Luzzatto, L., and P. Goodfellow. "A Simple Disease with No Cure." *Nature* 337 (1989): 17–18.

Manley, Audrey F. "Legislation and Funding for Sickle Cell Services, 1972–1982." *The American Journal of Pediatric Hematology/Oncology* 6 (1984): 67–71.

Markel, Howard. "Scientific Advances and Social Risks: Historical Perspectives of Genetic Screening Programs for Sickle Cell Disease, Tay-Sachs Disease, Neural Tube Defects and Down Syndrome, 1970–1997," in *Promoting Safe and Effective Genetic Testing in the United States*. National Human Genome Research Institute Web site. Available online. URL: http://www.genome.gov/10002401.

Marotta, Charles A., John T. Wilson, Bernard G. Forget, and Sherman M. Weissman. "Human Beta-globin Messenger RNA." *The Journal of Biological Chemistry* 252 (1977): 5040–5053.

Mason, V.R. "Sickle Cell Anemia." *Journal of the American Medical Association* 79 (1922): 1318–1320.

Mayell, Hillary. "Three High-altitude Peoples, Three Adaptations to Thin Air," National Geographic Web site. Available online. URL: http://news.nationalgeographic.com/news/2004/02/0224_040225_evolution.html.

Min-Oo, Gundula, and Philippe Gros. "Erythrocyte Variants and the Nature of Their Malaria Protective Effect." *Cellular Microbiology* 7 (2005): 753–763.

Near, Thomas J., Sandra K. Parker, and H. William Detrich III. "A Genomic Fossil Reveals Key Steps in Hemoglobin Loss by the Antarctic Icefishes." *Molecular Biology and Evolution* 23 (2006): 2008–2016.

Nucci, Mary L., and Abraham Abuchowski. "The Search for Blood Substitutes." *Scientific American* 278 (1998): 72–77.

Pauling, Linus, Harvey A. Itano, S.J. Singer, and Ibert C. Wells. "Sickle Cell Anemia, a Molecular Disease." *Science* 110 (1949): 543–548.

Pawliuk, Robert, Karen A. Westerman, Mary E. Fabry, Emmanuel Payen, Robert Tighe, Eric E. Bouhassira, Seetharama A. Acharya et al. "Correction of Sickle Cell Disease in Transgenic Mouse Models by Gene Therapy." *Science* 294 (2001): 2368–2371.

Pier, Gerald B., Martha Grout, Tanweer Zaidi, Gloria Meluleni, Simone S. Mueschenborn, George Banting, Rosemary Ratcliff, Martin J. Evans, and William H. Colledge. "*Salmonella typhi* Uses CFTR to Enter Intestinal Epithelial Cells." *Nature* 393 (1998): 79–82.

Rincon, Paul. "DNA 'Could Predict Your Surname'," BBC News Web site. Available online. URL: http://news.bbc.co.uk/2/hi/science/nature/4736984.stm.

Rogers, Z.R. "Review: Clinical Transfusion Management in Sickle Cell Disease." *Immunohematology* 22 (2006): 126–131.

Ruud, Johan T. "Vertebrates Without Erythrocytes and Blood Pigment." *Nature* 173 (1954): 848–850.

Sadelain, Michel. "Recent Advances in Globin Gene Transfer for the Treatment of Beta-thalassemia and Sickle Cell Anemia." *Current Opinion in Hematology* 13 (2006): 142–148.

Savitt, Todd L. "The Invisible Malady: Sickle Cell Anemia in America, 1910–1970." *Journal of the National Medical Association* 73 (1981): 739–746.

Savitt, Todd L. "The Second Reported Case of Sickle Cell Anemia: Charlottesville, Virginia, 1911." *Virginia Medical Quarterly* 124 (Spring 1997): 84–92.

Savitt, Todd L., and Morton F. Goldenberg. "Herrick's 1910 Case Report of Sickle Cell Anemia: The Rest of the Story." *Journal of the American Medical Association* 261 (1989): 266–271.

Schenker, Joseph G. "Ethical Aspects of Advanced Reproductive Technologies." *Annals of the New York Academy of Sciences* 997 (2003): 11–21.

Secretariat of the World Health Organization. "Sickle-cell Anaemia," WHO Web site. Available online. URL: http://www.who.int/gb/ebwha/pdf_files/WHA59/A59_9-en.pdf.

Serjeant, Graham R. "The Emerging Understanding of Sickle Cell Disease." *British Journal of Haematology* 112 (2001): 3–18.

Shreeve, James. "Genetic Trails Left by Our Ancestors Are Leading Scientists Back Across Time in An Epic Discovery of Human Migration," National Geographic Web site. Available online. URL: http://www7.nationalgeographic.com/ngm/0603/feature2/index.html.

Strachan, Tom, and Andrew Read. *Human Molecular Genetics,* 3rd ed. London: Garland Science Publishing, 2003.

Stray-Gundersen, J., R.F. Chapman, and B.D. Levine. "'Living High–Training Low' Altitude Training Improves Sea Level Performance in Male and Female Elite Runners." *Journal of Applied Physiology* 91 (2001): 1113–1120.

Stuart, Marie J., and Ronald L. Nagel. "Sickle-cell Disease." *Lancet* 364 (2004): 1343–1360.

Swerdlow, Paul S. "Red Cell Exchange in Sickle Cell Disease." *Hematology* 2006: 48–53.

Taliaferro, W.H., and J.G. Huck. "The Inheritance of Sickle-Cell Anaemia in Man." *Genetics* 8 (1923): 594–598.

Tanser, Paul H. "Biology of the Heart and Blood Vessels." In *The Merck Manual of Medical Information, Second Home Edition*, edited by Mark H. Beers, 114–118. West Point, PA: Merck & Company, Inc., 2003.

Taylor, Todd D., Hideki Noguchi, Yasushi Totoki, Atsushi Toyoda, Yoko Kuroki, Ken Dewar, Christine Lloyd et al. "Human Chromosome 11 DNA Sequence and Analysis Including Novel Gene Identification." *Nature* 440 (2006): 497–500.

"T-Boz Speaks Out in PSA to Help People with SCD," Sickle Cell Disease Association of America, Inc. Web site. Available online. URL: http://www.sicklecelldisease.org/info/spokesperson_tboz.phtml.

"Thalassemia," March of Dimes Web site. Available online. URL: http://www.marchofdimes.com

Thompson, Larry. "Human Gene Therapy: Harsh Lessons, High Hopes," FDA Web site. Available online. URL: http://www.fda.gov/fdac/features/2000/500_gene.html.

Trivedi, Bijal P. "Gene Therapy Used to Treat Sickle Cell Disease in Mice." National Geographic Web Site. Available online. URL: http://news.nationalgeographic.com/news/2001/12/1213_TVsickle.html.

"Understanding Vaccines," National Institute of Allergy and Infectious Diseases Web site. Available online. URL: http://www.niaid.nih.gov/publications/vaccine/undvacc.htm.

Wailoo, Keith. *Dying in the City of the Blues*. Chapel Hill: The University of North Carolina Press, 2001.

Wailoo, Keith, and Stephen Pemberton. *The Troubled Dream of Genetic Medicine*. Baltimore: The Johns Hopkins University Press, 2006.

Walker, Matthew R., and Ralph Rapley. *Route Maps in Gene Technology*. Oxford, UK: Blackwell Science Ltd., 1997.

Walters, Mark C. "Stem Cell Therapy for Sickle Cell Disease: Transplantation and Gene Therapy." *Hematology* (2005): 66–73.

Watkins, Tionne. "SCDAA Spokesperson: Tionne 'T-Boz' Watkins," Sickle Cell Disease Association of America, Inc. Web site. Available online. URL: http://www.sicklecelldisease. org/info/spokesperson.phtml.

Weatherall, D.J., and J.B. Clegg. "Inherited Haemoglobin Disorders: An Increasing Global Health Problem." *Bulletin of the World Health Organization* 79 (2001): 704–712.

Weatherall, David, Olu Akinyanju, Suthat Fucharoen, Nancy Olivieri, and Philip Musgrove. "Inherited Disorders of Hemoglobin." In *Disease Control Priorities in Developing Countries,* 2nd ed., edited by Dean T. Jamison, Joel G. Breman, Anthony R. Measham, George Alleyne, Mariam Claeson, David B. Evans, Prabhat Jha, Anne Mills, and Philip Musgrove, 663–680. New York: Oxford University Press, 2006.

Wethers, Doris L. "Sickle Cell Disease in Childhood," American Academy of Family Physicians Web site. Available online. URL: http://www.aafp.org/afp/20000901/1013.html.

"What Is Tay-Sachs Disease," National Tay-Sachs & Allied Diseases Association, Inc. Web site. Available online. URL: http://www.ntsad.org/S02/S02tay_sachs.htm.

"What Is Thalassemia?" Cooley's Anemia Foundation Web site. Available online. URL: http://www.cooleysanemia.org/ sections.php?sec=1.

Williams, Precious. "The Doctors Told Me I Wouldn't Live to See 40." *Evening Standard* (London), November 27, 2002.

Wu, Li-Chen, Chiao-Wang Sun, Thomas M. Ryan, Kevin M. Pawlik, Jinxiang Ren, and Tim M. Townes. "Correction of Sickle Cell Disease by Homologous Recombination in Embryonic Stem Cells." *Blood* 108 (2006): 1183–1188.

FURTHER READING

Boudreau, Gloria. *The Immune System*. San Diego: KidHaven Press, 2004.

Claybourne, Anna. *Introduction to Genes and DNA*. London: Usborne Publishing Limited, 2003.

Davidson, Sue, and Ben Morgan. *Human Body Revealed*. New York: DK Publishing, 2002.

Fridell, Ron. *Decoding Life: Unraveling the Mysteries of the Genome*. Minneapolis: Lerner Publishing Group, 2004.

Morris, Jonathan. *The Ethics of Biotechnology*. New York: Chelsea House Publishers, 2005.

Panno, Joseph. *Gene Therapy*. New York: Chelsea House Publishers, 2004.

Panno, Joseph. *Stem Cell Research*. New York: Chelsea House Publishers, 2004.

Phelan, Glen. *Double Helix*. Washington, DC: National Geographic Children's Books, 2006.

Schacter, Bernice. *Biotechnology and Your Health*. New York: Chelsea House Publishers, 2005.

Snedden, Robert. *DNA and Genetic Engineering*. Chicago: Heinemann, 2002.

Walker, Richard. *Genes and DNA*. New York: Houghton Mifflin Company, 2003.

Whittemore, Susan. *The Circulatory System*. New York: Chelsea House Publishers, 2003.

WEB SITES

GeneTests

http://www.genetests.org/

Funded by the National Institutes of Health, this public resource provides information on genetic testing and counseling, and also hosts a directory of genetics clinics.

Genetic Disease Profile: Sickle Cell Anemia

http://www.ornl.gov/sci/techresources/Human_Genome/posters/chromosome/sca.shtml

The Gene Gateway profile page for sickle cell anemia includes an overview of the disease, linking to further information about the HBB gene. The profile also features a timeline of historical events leading up to the current knowledge about sickle cell disease.

National Heart, Lung, and Blood Institute—Diseases and Conditions Index

http://www.nhlbi.nih.gov/health/dci/index.html

This easily searchable index of heart, lung, blood, and sleep disorders is intended as a resource for public education about causes, symptoms, and treatments of a broad range of illnesses.

Online Mendelian Inheritance in Man

http://www.ncbi.nlm.nih.gov/entrez/query.fcgi?db=OMIM

A searchable database supported by Johns Hopkins University that allows users to search for information about human genes and genetic disorders

Sickle Cell Disease Association of America, Inc.

http://www.sicklecelldisease.org/index.phtml

A national organization that promotes funding for sickle cell research, outreach and support to those with the sickle cell disease, and public education about the disease

The Sickle Cell Information Center

http://www.scinfo.org/index.htm

The mission of the Sickle Cell Information Center includes the goal of eliminating sickle cell disease through education, research, and the right level of care. The website contains a broad range of resources, from information on newborn screening to details about pharmaceuticals and blood donations.

Sickle Cell Society

http://www.sicklecellsociety.org/index.htm

A charitable organization that provides outreach to sickle cell patients in need of medical treatment

PICTURE CREDITS

INDEX

stem cells
  bone marrow, 105, 107
  cord blood, 97–98
  embryonic, 105–106,
    114–115
  genetically modified,
    105–109
  nonembryonic, 105–106
  pluripotential, 36
stroke, 57
sugar-phosphate backbone, 24
surnames, Y chromosome
  genetic markers and, 80–81
symptoms, 17–18, 54–59, 86
synthetic genes, 31
synthetic polymers, 25

T

Tatum, Edward, 30
Tay-Sachs disease, 89–90
thalassemia, 42–43
Thirteenth Amendment, 8
thymine, 27, 32
transcription, 33
transgenes, 99–100, 104
translation, 33
treatments
  blood transfusions, 91–92,
    97
  bone marrow transplants,
    92–96, 97
  cord blood stem cells,
    98–99
  drug, 88–91
  ethical concerns with,
    111–115

gene therapy, 99–109,
    111–114
  genetically modified stem
    cells, 105–109
  potential, 97–109
trypsin, 41
typhoid fever, 99

U

United States, number with
  sickle cell disease in,
    17, 60
uracil, 32, 33
urea, 111

V

vaccines, 95–96, 111
valine, 42, 45
vaso-occlusion, 51–52,
    53, 59
vector DNA, 108
veins, 50, 51, 52
viruses, 100, 104, 113

W

Washburn, Benjamin Earl, 11
Watkins, Tionne, 13
Watson, James, 30, 32
white blood cells, 93–94

X

X chromosomes, 66

Y

Y chromosome, 66,
    80–81

ABOUT THE AUTHOR

Phill Jones earned a PhD in physiology/pharmacology from the University of California, San Diego. After completing postdoctoral training at Stanford University School of Medicine, he joined the Department of Biochemistry at the University of Kentucky Medical Center as an assistant professor, where he taught topics in molecular biology and medicine and researched aspects of gene expression. He later earned a JD at the University of Kentucky College of Law and worked ten years as a patent attorney, specializing in biological, chemical, and medical inventions. Dr. Jones is now a full-time writer. His science-based articles have appeared in *Today's Science on File*, *The World Almanac and Book of Facts*, *Forensic Magazine*, *Genomics and Proteomics Magazine*, *Forensic Nurse Magazine*, *Nature Biotechnology*, *Information Systems for Biotechnology News Report*, *Law and Order Magazine*, *PharmaTechnology Magazine*, and Florida Department of Education publications. He is also a regular contributor to *History Magazine*.